DAMAGE NOTED ___ scribbling this page

DATE 9/28/10 BRANCH ___ STAFF INITIALS IC

Make a
Name for
Yourself

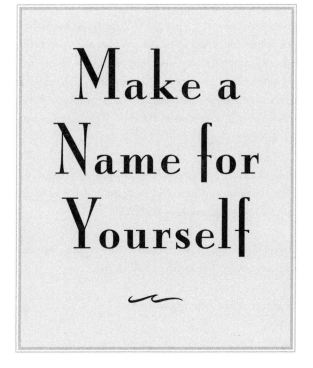

Make a Name for Yourself

Robin Fisher Roffer

BROADWAY BOOKS

NEW YORK

BROADWAY

Broadway Books titles may be purchased for business or promotional use or for special sales. For information, please write to: Special Markets Department, Random House, Inc., 1540 Broadway, New York, NY 10036.

BROADWAY BOOKS and its logo, a letter B bisected on the diagonal, are trademarks of Broadway Books, a division of Random House, Inc.

Visit our Web site at www.broadwaybooks.com

Library of Congress Cataloging-in-Publication Data

Roffer, Robin Fisher, 1962–
Make a name for yourself / Robin Fisher Roffer
with Doris Ober.—1st ed.
p.   cm.
1. Women—Life skills guides. 2. Women—Identity.
3. Self-realization. 4. Success. 5. Career development.
I. Title.
HQ1221 .R68 2000
646.7'0082—dc21   00-036040

FIRST EDITION

Designed by Lee Fukui

ISBN 0-7679-0491-5

00   01   02   03   04   10   9   8   7   6   5   4   3   2   1

Contents

Introduction
1

STEP 1:
Dig Deep to Unearth
Who You Are
11

STEP 2:
Define Your Dreams and
Put Them into Action
39

STEP 3:

Go After Your Target Audience
with a Vengeance
61

STEP 4:

Don't Crash and Burn—
Figure Out What's Stopping You
87

STEP 5:

Recruit a Squad of
Brand Cheerleaders
113

STEP 6:

Learn the Secrets to
Packaging Your Brand
133

STEP 7:

Get Comfortable in
Your Own Skin
159

STEP 8:

Devise a Plan and
Get on with It
183

CONCLUSION:
The Next Step
209

Notes
211

Acknowledgments
213

About the Author
215

Introduction

The idea of using branding techniques as a way to identify and establish yourself in the business world hit me like a ton of bricks at a trade show cocktail party. It was one of those evenings where everyone in your field is there trying to impress everybody else and networking like crazy.

Suddenly a television bigwig appeared at my elbow with an important client in tow. "Robin!" said the host, enthusiastically. "I want you to meet George!" Then he turned to George. "George!" he exclaimed. "This is Robin Fisher, the Sweepstakes Queen of Cable!" Huge smile on his face.

I nearly dropped my drink. I'd never thought of myself as a Sweepstakes Queen, not even when I worked sweepstakes exclusively. Wasn't I a whole lot more than that? Was Sweepstakes Queen how *everybody* thought of me?

Without knowing it had happened, I had been *branded,* and branded as someone I didn't want to be. After I got over the initial shock, it taught me an important lesson:

If you don't brand yourself, someone else will.

This book gives you the tools to brand yourself before someone else does it to you—or to change your brand if it doesn't reflect your true self. *Whether you're an artist or an accountant—whatever your field; whether you work for a company or for yourself; whether you're out looking for a job, or looking to advance yourself in your career, or looking to change careers—this book gives you control over how you're perceived.* After all, positive differentiation in a sea of sameness is the key to career success.

This book shares many of the branding strategies that work successfully for big corporate entities in establishing or promoting their particular brand, whether it's Coca-Cola, Nike, or MTV. But in these pages *you are the brand.*

Your goal will be to let your brand become a vehicle for your most authentic self. In this way you'll distinguish yourself from others who do similar work, affirm your true identity, highlight your talents, and establish your reputation in business. Reinforcing your brand, practicing brand consistency, will cause people to respond to you just as you'd like them to, so that when they hear your name mentioned they make positive associations. Eventually a trusted brand earns customer loyalty. You can expect the same.

If anyone knows this truth, I do. I've been a brand strategist for some of the best and brightest cable networks: TNT, CNN, Discovery Channel, Lifetime Television, ESPN, A&E, and MTV, as well as digital giants like IBM and America Online. My company, Big Fish Marketing, has launched nine national and global television brands, and numerous Web sites; but in the beginning, in the early 1990s, I sold sweepstakes ideas to television networks. "Watch the Discovery Channel and win a Safari adventure!" That sort of thing. It was fun work, even if it wasn't the most glamorous job, and it put me where I wanted to be—in a world where just about everybody loved TV as much as I did.

I made branding my specialty just as it was beginning to be applied to television as a way to differentiate the ever-increasing number of cable channels. Today branding has become so valuable in product success that brand strategists like myself now exist in almost every type of industry and work with almost every type of product, from soft drinks to large appliances, from electronic services to resort hotels. Even countries qualify for branding. In the summer of 1999, Prime Minister Tony Blair kicked off a national campaign to brand England. Casting off its Elizabethan image, England was going to enter the twenty-first century as "Cool Brittania," land of the Spice Girls and Austin Powers.

Of course we've had "brands" of marketable items for a long time. But only recently has a brand become more than just a mark, or a word, or a logo that manufacturers put on their appliances, packaged goods, or services to identify them.

Today the manufacturer itself may be the brand, the whole supermarket is a brand, and so are TV stations and networks, movies, and Web sites. For a company, the brand represents its word, its message, even its reason for being, as well as its badge of honor—and branding has become the process of endowing the company and the product with all of that. When people recognize a brand name they actually have an emotional response to the name. They know immediately what the product is. They may have confidence in its quality, or at least an opinion about its value. They may become loyal (or at least dependable) customers or they may prefer another brand entirely. We *identify* a product by and with its brand.

The day after that fateful cocktail party, I set out to change my brand.

I wanted my identity in my career to be a better representation of me than "Sweepstakes Queen." I wanted my name to be identified with my core values, and my passions, and the person I am inside. I intuitively understood that this was going to be a big commitment. If I wanted to become the person I would be proud to be I would have to begin to reflect my values and passions and my authentic self in everything I did—in my word, message, action, and style—from then on. I had ambition and energy, I was thirty-two and relatively established in my career, and I had some very big dreams. So I created a brand strategy for myself—one designed to reveal the genuine Robin Fisher.

First I focused on who I am. If not a "Sweepstakes Queen," then what concise descriptive phrase could I come up with that would sum me up? I asked myself: What is unique about me? What are my talents? What do I do that distinguishes me from the crowd? Then I looked at my dreams. What kind of success am I looking for? What precisely do I want for myself and my future? And then, who is my "target audience"—that is, who do I want to impress and do business with? Who will help me fulfill my dreams? And finally, how could I package and promote myself to achieve these goals?

I'll give you an example of how branding, mostly thought of as an application process—something put on externally—is actually a process that opens a window to the soul of the product being branded.

In the winter of 1991 I was a marketing executive at Turner Broadcasting. We were trying to work up an advertising campaign for CNN to capitalize on its coverage of Desert Storm. It was the network's first big promotional drive. It was also the first time *live* war footage had ever been available to anyone who wanted to watch. I was in New York for a conference and ended up glued to my TV set. Bombs were falling in Baghdad, and I was following it, live on CNN, from my hotel room. I couldn't turn it off. It was amazing to me that I could watch the war *as it happened, twenty-four hours a day.* I felt as if the whole world must be watching, too.

Back in Atlanta we talked about that feeling of global awe. All of us felt it. We went to our ad agency and asked if they could do something with the concept of the whole world watching.

In a few days the ad agency came back with a poster. It was a NASA shot of the earth from outer space. And above the image were the words "Watch what happens next." A bold CNN logo signed off the message.

It took my breath away. I always know a good idea because the hair stands up on my arms, and it was doing it then. There was no picture of Baghdad or of bombs, no soldiers, no blood. The image and the words were all about the war, but they transcended CNN's war coverage. The photo and the caption said that CNN was much more than its coverage of Desert Storm.

At the same time, CNN was kicking around ideas for a tagline—those little words you see under the logo, like a motto. Building on the "big idea" that the whole world watches CNN, we added the line "The World's News Leader" to the poster and to all of our advertising for the Gulf War coverage.

In a very short time, those words became a self-fulfilling prophecy. Soon we heard the Secretary of Defense, Dick Cheney, saying, "We want to thank the folks at CNN for bringing the war to us every day so we can keep up with what's going on in Baghdad." And I can still hear Peter Jennings's inflection when he said about CNN: "It used to be called the little network that could . . . but not anymore!" (Actually, it was called the "chicken noodle news" by the other networks. But not anymore!)

CNN's image had evolved from a small, locally produced news channel to the most trusted and reliable news source on television. Today people all over the globe recognize those initials, know what kind of programs CNN produces, and feel confident about the quality of those programs. And the network has a large audience of loyal (or at least dependable) viewers who turn to CNN for live, breaking coverage of major news events.

Branding for people is about finding *your* "big idea," the core you, and putting it out in the universe to fulfill itself. For example, look at how her core values are reflected in Oprah Winfrey's brand:

BACKGROUND

From her earliest years, Oprah showed a talent for talking to groups of people. Hardship, human frailty, women's issues shaped her childhood, all things she learned from experience or observation as a very little girl. These were the issues that formed her, and they are the issues she pursues today with such passion. Oprah is who she is, which is at the very heart and soul of her brand. For the same reason, is it any wonder that her book club is so incredibly successful? Her love, admiration, interest, and connection with books were learned at her grandma's knee and affirmed and nurtured by her dad. Oprah's book club is a celebration of the value she herself places on books.

BRAND DESCRIPTION

Role model, mentor, and girlfriend, Oprah is bounty personified. She is wealthy. She is generous. She demonstrates her largesse in body and soul. She's a giver, out there, frank, one hundred percent, not mincing words, sharing what she's got, what she thinks and feels, what's important to her. Spirituality is important to her, and she puts that out there, too, using a talk show milieu for stimulating discussions that dare to tap into our spiritual selves without going completely over the edge.

PERSONALITY/ATTITUDE

Oprah is	*Oprah is not*
serious	frivolous
outgoing	self-centered
honest	duplicitous
generous	stingy
vulnerable	hard
energetic	laid-back
warm	cold

Key Attributes

- Focused determination

- Her market influence is awesome. Thirty million people totally trust her. She is truly beloved.

Packaging

- Physically attractive with strong features, beautifully groomed, dark hair kept soft around her face.

- Except for a little more makeup, she doesn't look too much different than the members of her audience.

- Clothes are sometimes bold colors, usually monochromatic outfits, always tailored to flatter her fluctuating weight.

Presentation

- Straightforwardness, soulfulness, and concern are hallmarks of Oprah's presentation. You can hear it in her voice, see it on her face, and read it in her eyes.

- She's an "in front of the podium" person. She likes to create an intimate connection with her audience.

- Communicates inner power and beauty with *no pretense,* making her attractive to women in all walks of life.

Mission Statement

To help people lead better lives.

The shorthand above is a way of focusing on one aspect of brand building at a time. It's a method you'll see repeated throughout the book, and one you'll use to help identify and understand the power of your own brand.

Success is the subtext for this book about branding, so I want to be clear about what I mean by success. I'm talking about *success in the workplace,* as symbolized by financial reward and/or professional respect. But I'm also talking about self-actualization. The process of branding allows you to become the person you are meant to be. Branding makes you an active partner in fulfilling your destiny in business and in life.

Branding is also gender-friendly. Men can use it, too. But I've written this book for women because, of the many books for career success in bookstores today, I haven't found many that resonate with a woman's emotional experience in striving to get ahead in work. Without getting into all the chemical explanations for it, let's just say that we'd rather not be at war with people who happen to be in competition with us. Intimidation is not usually comfortable for us—either side of it. We don't want to fight or connive to keep a client or a job. And we don't want to have to dress in armor to survive in the workplace.

Branding is a technique for success that doesn't use weapons or combat or camouflage. Instead of arms, building a personal brand strategy lets us wield our truest selves. Instead of an assault on the marketplace, we come bearing the gift of our own best qualities, packaged in a way to attract precisely the people who need us, and want us, and will appreciate us most.

Women desire success as much as any man—just not at the expense of our unique emotional value systems or our spiritual selves—not in business, not in life. Most women I know in the corporate world are about cooperation and balance. It's in our nature to seek consensus, to promote peace, and yet we often end up trading personal fulfillment, joy, or generosity for prosperity. And we shouldn't have to.

Today's working women are waking up to their spiritual need to live authentically, to be true to their heart's desires and their moral sensibilities, to feel a sense of purpose and fulfillment, and to feel right with their path and how they navigate that path. These are *my* desires and sensibilities, too, and these precepts are at the heart of what branding offers.

The branding process consists of eight steps, the first of which is one of self-discovery, in which you'll develop a brand description, subjecting yourself, as if you were a product, to the same meticulous review that I'd do for America Online, Comedy Central, or ESPN—beginning with such questions as: "What does *Brand Me* do? What are the best things about it? What do I want people to think when they hear my (brand) name? What reputation do I want my brand to develop?" I think you'll find that being able to step back and evaluate yourself as a brand is at least as interesting as the more traditional, deeply psychological ways we sometimes try to gain self-knowledge.

Once you've got a handle on your brand identity and your aspirations, I offer a course in how to find and win your target audience. Then you'll put a magnifying lens on what holds you back and what dangers lurk in the shadows of life at work. You'll learn how to find a mentor, secrets of brand packaging, and methods of presentation, and I'll show you how to design a business plan for yourself as well as an ongoing program for care and maintenance.

At the end of every chapter I've included a summary section that asks you to record your personal responses to the prompts and questions in the chapters. From the answers to these questions you should be able to build a brand strategy that's absolutely suited to you and to no one else. I recommend transcribing these summary sections into a "brand planner" or career journal (outlined in Step Eight) so that you can continue to monitor your brand's progress, your professional growth, even after you've finished this book.

Throughout the book I've shared stories from my experiences in business, in addition to those of friends and colleagues. In all cases, the stories are true, but in several cases I've changed the names of characters, or their companies, or otherwise disguised an event or situation in order to preserve an individual's or company's privacy or anonymity.

In the four branding stories you'll follow throughout the book, each is based on a real person whose situation is as I've described it, but I've also taken some liberties. I've added certain details and made demographic alterations in the lives of the four women in order to make their stories emblematic of stories that many women can relate to, no matter what their type of business, whether they're working for a big company or on their own, whether they're just starting out or have their eye fixed on the CEO's corner office and all that comes with it.

I believe in both miracles and destiny, but in the end we make our own realities. Branding doesn't happen just by deciding it's a good idea. There's a lot of work to do in the pages that follow, and it's a process that will take time. So why should you bother? Here's why: To know who you are and be valued for it, to attract what you want, to become more attractive to others, to inspire confidence, to walk your path with integrity, and to distinguish yourself in whatever field you've chosen.

Dig Deep to Unearth Who You Are

I believe that we're here in the world for a purpose. Everything that happens to us, good or bad, is a lesson to help us discover what that purpose is and fulfill it. This is the real business of life, our destiny cycle, played out in our love life and our work life.

Your true purpose can only be discovered when you've looked deeply and honestly into your heart and allowed the true you to declare herself. She may be someone very different from the you that other people see today, but *she* is the soul of your brand and it's with her help above all others that you'll find your path and your success. When you've discovered her you can begin to honor her by revealing her dynamic spirit to the world. She will reward you with everything you ever dreamed was possible.

What words come to mind when people say your name? What do people *feel* when they see you? If you can't answer these questions easily, join the club. How can you ever know what someone else is thinking, anyway? And after all, how objective can you really be about yourself?

The truth is you *can* know what people are thinking about you if you've put certain thoughts in their heads.

What's the Buzz on You?

I'm not talking about mind control exactly, but branding *is* about having a strong influence over how you're perceived. Look how the best brands bombard us on a daily basis with in-your-face advertising designed to influence how we think and feel about their products. Coca-Cola wants us to think "refreshing" when we hear their name, and to make sure we do they spend big dollars to promote their brand as invigorating and exhilarating. Disney's name is indelibly associated with family values and wholesome kid entertainment. MTV has influenced us to think of hip young people and cutting-edge music. Think Volvo, think safety. Think Jeep, think adventure.

Apply brand promotion to people and you get similar results. For instance, what words come to mind when you think of Madonna? How about Oprah? Or Martha Stewart? Not too long ago, I asked a group of women in the film industry to describe these powerful women, and they came up with these three lists.

organized	outrageous	compassionate
creative	sexy	spiritual
anal	chameleon	intelligent
intimidating	brassy	genuine

It's not too hard to guess which list applies to which celebrity, is it? That's because in marketing terms, all three women are super powerful brands. Their names evoke a strong, even emotional response from us, and we pretty much know what to expect from each of them, which is why we remember them. They're consistent.

Consistency is one of branding's most important laws. Madonna, Oprah, and Martha build their brands by making career choices that reinforce what they're known for. Madonna changes her look almost as often as Oprah chooses another book or Martha recovers a sofa. Oprah continues to make women aware of issues that matter, and we'll never see Martha put out anything short of domestic perfection. Madonna has made *extreme* inconsistency a part of her brand—changing from the blond bombshell she personified during and around the filming of the movie *Dick Tracy* with Warren Beatty in 1990, to the raven-haired Indian gurette in exotic saris of 1999. Doing so, she's pretty much locked in to being consistently inconsistent. I don't recommend this. Brand *consistency* is critical to developing brand loyalty. Brand inconsistency erodes confidence. And so Madonna's "chameleon" quality may ultimately undermine her success. She may never be able to rest or stop changing because if she did, her audience would get bored.

Consistency, clarity, and authenticity are the
holy trinity of a great brand.

When I'm hired to help a cable network or Internet company develop its brand, I begin by analyzing the brand's distinguishing qualities, its key attributes, its defining characteristics. If I were doing a brand analysis of Martha and Madonna, for instance, they would look something like this:

Martha Stewart

BRAND DESCRIPTION

Goddess of her own Omnimedia empire (magazine, syndicated column, and TV show), Martha reigns supreme over every avenue of domesticity: home crafts, home decor, and home entertaining. Worth billions now that she's gone public, her ubiquitous presence is secure for the rest of her baking years and beyond. Martha does everything right, she does it meticulously, and she's strict—she doesn't fool around and she expects us to do as she does. You either love her or hate her.

VALUES

Her core values reflect her quest for perfection, and her love of the best and the beautiful. They play to the new American dream of homemaking: More is better—and you have to admit, it all looks great!

KEY ATTRIBUTES

- Vision coupled with flawless taste
- A love for detail that makes something as mundane as repositioning the sofa seem fascinating
- An in-charge personality

PACKAGING

Down-to-earth looks, lots of slacks, overalls, gardening clogs, button-up blouses, barn jackets, minimal make up; simple, short hair style. A very casual low-maintenance look balances a very highly contrived product.

BRAND POWER

- Martha at Kmart—'nuf said
- Soaring stock valuations
- Women all over America are captivated by her and the world she's created

TAGLINE

"It's a good thing!"

POSITIONING:

The last word in American of home crafts, decor, and entertaining

BOTTOM LINE

Her arrogance is legion, her attitude intimidating, her taste and talent enviable.

Madonna

BRAND DESCRIPTION

Innovative, influential, and inspiring, a singer, dancer, composer, producer, actor, executive, humanitarian, and mother, Madonna is embedded in our pop culture and collective consciousness as an icon for the liberated, highly physical, sexual female. Always an original, sometimes outrageous, she's never shy about showing us exactly who she is.

KEY ATTRIBUTES

- Dazzling, alluring, in-your-face!

- She brings together music, extravagant theatrics, and dance to wow sold-out audiences around the world.

- Touches something primal in us—evokes extreme emotional response.

- She has more than confidence—she has guts. She pushes the envelope.

- An original creative vision and the ability to pick up on and set trends in everything from fashion to design to music.

BRAND POWER

- She sells records! No less than nineteen top ten singles in the past fourteen years, eleven of them number one.

- Her influence on fashion is revolutionary.

- Recognizing the creative and commercial impact of the music video lexicon, no one has done more to marry music and image.

QUOTE

"I live faster than everyone else . . . out of my own curiosity and hunger for information and change."

WHAT PEOPLE THINK OF MADONNA

She's a great marketer.

WHAT PEOPLE ARE MISSING

She's an astonishing talent and a reflection of what many women secretly aspire to be. And that scares a lot of people.

These analyses aren't identical in their content because branding isn't done with a cookie cutter, but the process is one that can be duplicated, no matter what or who the brand. Martha, Madonna, and Oprah have created their own personal successes in just the same way any other successful brand does—by focusing on who they are and what is unique about them, on who they want to reach and how they want to be thought of, and by packaging and promoting themselves to accomplish their goals.

Your brand's success is achieved in the same way. The very first step is to *model your brand on your authentic self*. There's only one like it in the world, which makes it (1) distinct from any other and (2) something you and only you can pull off.

To do this you must dig deep to know who you are, what you stand for, and what you believe in.

Mary Beth

At age twenty-eight, Mary Beth thought she was finally getting a handle on that age-old question "Who am I?"—and it was neither the privileged southern debutante or the Yuppie corporate drone that her parents thought she should be. Mary Beth was different—always had been. When she was seven, she transformed her mother's favorite tablecloth into a giant jigsaw puzzle. In eighth grade she had used her watercolors to dye her light-colored hair purple. She had flair. And as an adult, she had far greater ambitions than what the account management ladder offered at Grey Advertising, which was the path her family was aggressively encouraging her to follow.

Mary Beth had graduated from Emory University in Atlanta with a communications degree, earned an MBA at Kellogg, and then moved to Manhattan with a girlfriend. Her first job out had been with Grey as an account coordinator. She worked for them for several years, but she had no passion for account work, and she believed that traditional agencies like Grey were wanna-bes in the media revolution, no longer fully equipped to serve clients. Besides, her salary was uninspiring compared to what many of her classmates at Kellogg were earning by now. And salary was important to Mary Beth.

She knew intuitively that the money would come if she could reposition herself from a "suit" to a "creative," so ignoring her parents' gloomy predictions, she left Grey and enrolled at the prestigious Parsons School of Design.

See Yourself as a Brand

Even without a physical description of Mary Beth, you begin to get a picture of her, and a sense of her courage and determination to work at something that resonates with who she is and what she stands for. But it's not always so easy to define those two essential elements. So here's a game I play with women who attend my workshops to get them thinking about these kinds of existential questions. I ask:

You are a product: What are you, and why?

Without my prompting, the answer to this question is invariably a product with a well-known brand name, and the answer to "why" almost always incorporates the brand's tagline, that short, upbeat phrase that everyone associates with the brand. No one says "chicken soup." They say, "I'm Knorr's Chicken Bouillon—because I add flavor to everything." They don't say "champagne," but "Veuve Clicquot—because I'm bubbly, expensive, and enjoyed by people with the very best taste." They don't say they're a "car," but a "BMW—because I'm the ultimate driving machine!"

Notice that the justifications in these objectives are all positive statements. "I add flavor . . ." "I'm bubbly . . ." "I'm the ultimate . . ." In this game, you want to be thinking in the most positive terms about yourself. Branding is positive by nature. It will bring out the best in you.

But not all of us are 100 percent perky, "up with people," everything-is-rosy optimists. In being true to our authentic selves, should we pretend there is no darker side?

Don't let this be a moral dilemma. *Never* play the victim in business. Never play a loser, or a weakling, or a bad guy just to get a reaction. "Never let them see you sweat," as my dad says.

Even though we *do* sweat. Even though loss is an inevitable part of life. Even though sometimes we *are* weak, and sometimes we're not as nice as we should have been. It's usually a good idea to differentiate your professional life from your private life. It's rarely in a brand's best interest to "tell all," nor should it be necessary.

Maybe you're competent and dedicated and highly skilled in your line of work, but you had a difficult childhood and you're emotionally vulnerable. Or you're basically an angry person, or you're depressed. These are not assets at work and they won't contribute to the success of your brand—in fact, they can become obstacles to success if they're not kept in check. There's a difference between honoring your authentic self and sharing your personal truth, and moaning, complaining, and being explosive.

Spend some time thinking of a brand you can identify with. Brands come in categories, so start by deciding what classification you could fit. Are you a food product, providing sustenance to people? And if so, what kind of food: crisp, smooth, liquid, solid, new, improved? Do any of these adjectives speak to you?

Are you an appliance that's the top of its line, technologically? Is that appliance practical or extravagant, electric or battery-run, high tech, hand-held, or digital? Do any of these descriptive phrases contain an element you can relate to—on any level? Try to make your brand, and your reason for resonating with that brand, as specific and detailed as possible. The details will tell us much about the meaning beyond the brand name.

Maybe you're a fashion brand: Does Versace describe you, or are you a J. Crew type? Or do you identify with a media brand like CNN or MTV, or with a digital brand like AOL or Amazon.com? Your brand category might be a vehicle, or a financial institution, or a major metropolis. Brands come in all shapes and sizes. Any noun can be a brand.

When you've thought of a brand whose description seems to fit you personally, try substituting your name for the brand name. The workshop participant who said she was Knorr's Chicken Bouillon because she added flavor would now say: "I'm Kate Watkins. I add flavor to everything!" Or "I'm Lori Deck—bubbly, expensive, and enjoyed by people with the very best taste."

If you answered, "I'm a Maytag washing machine because I'm completely dependable and never break down," can you claim the same about yourself in real life?

Mary Beth

Influenced by the startling images of John Lennon and Yoko Ono, Albert Einstein, Alfred Hitchcock, and other visionaries that Apple Computer has associated with its brand in stark black-and-white billboards, Mary Beth aligned her personal brand with the company and its tagline. She wrote, "I'm Mary Beth, I 'think different.' "

If the brand you chose doesn't describe you accurately, keep trying. Find a brand that suits you better. By working at it, the exercise will reveal some of your essential ingredients, which we'll use to customize a brand description later in this chapter.

Search for the Soul of Your Brand

Like most successful brands, Apple reveals its soul in its advertising. It demonstrates its own visionary qualities—passion and creativity—in the extraordinary, far-thinking people it associates with its logo on those billboards. What words speak of *your* personal value system, that metronome for personal behavior—what you stand for, what you want to live up to, what you consider most important to your inner life and well-being?

Your values are integral to your brand qualities.

Mary Beth says she values money, courage, creativity, and vision. Kate Watkins at the workshop, who said she "adds flavor," may count diversity or the spice of life as one of her values. It's likely that Lori Deck, who said she was "bubbly," values fun and enthusiasm most of all. The workshop participant who called herself "the ultimate driving machine" could consider hard work and perseverance among her most cherished values.

Successful brands are built on core values and during their lifetimes constantly build on and reinforce their core values. They'll illustrate their values in their logo; they'll recite their values in their taglines; they'll promote their values in their public relations efforts.

Quaker Oats products want you to know that they stand for old-fashioned, homespun American goodness. Their logo uses that familiar, friendly looking traditional Quaker to personify those values. Everybody knows that Nike is a synonym for an active lifestyle. Their tagline, "Just do it!," says so. Pepsi Cola has revised its brand to showcase "joy" as in "The Joy of Cola," instead of the more difficult to describe values of "Generation Next," by which they had been known until recently. Home Depot, the largest retailer of lumber in the U.S., announced not long ago that it would no longer buy or sell lumber logged out of endangered forests. It wants its customers to know where its values lie. Volvo values safety above all, and advertises itself that way.

My values have to do with empowerment, integrity, and love. I feel the absolute best when these three values are operating in my life. I think I'm less than complete when any of them are compromised. I want to stand for these things and be known for them, and so I have to build these values into my brand.

I have another friend whose life is all about service—serving humanity, serving her family and community. When I think of her, I think of Mother Teresa, and I'm not the only one. This impression is part of her brand. I know another person who, like Coca-Cola, values being "the real thing" above all. Authenticity and honesty are what she identifies as her values, and it comes across loud and clear in the direct way she looks at you, in her no-nonsense responses, in her unselfconscious, refreshingly unpretentious manner.

The following list of words may help you identify what's deeply meaningful in your life. Use them to prompt yourself to recognize your own values.

Personal values

authenticity	generosity	honesty
success	love	kindness

loyalty	community	connectedness
courage	ethics	creativity
inspiration	appreciation	growth
good deeds	happiness	wisdom
warmth	adventure	contentment
knowledge	wealth	security
friendship	empathy	service
good humor	devotion	spirituality
morality	good health	having fun
family	freedom	commitment
open-mindedness	justice	tolerance
optimism	philanthropy	integrity

Of these, what do you consider to be your *core values,* that is, the three or four *most meaningful* to you? Which values do you live by? Which would you defend with your dying breath? In his True Leadership workshops, Sean Mason, a consultant to *Fortune* 500 companies, defines core values as "unique"—that is, they are based on your personal life experience. You and I may both list *integrity* as a core value, but it will mean something a little different for each of us. Core values are also "essential." That is you feel you couldn't live without them. And they are "universal," which means that they apply in all circumstances for you, all the time.

Now ask yourself these two questions:

How do I act out my core values every day?

How do I deny my value system?

For example, *love* is one of my core values. One of the ways I act out that value in my daily life is through my work, which I love; with my husband, whom I adore; and toward myself, by eating right and working out and keeping healthy. I would be denying these values if I began to take what's so precious to me for granted, got sloppy with my work, or my husband, or myself. Another of my core values is *empowerment,* and I act that out by cheerleading my clients, mentoring my co-workers, and giving myself no limits to meeting my potential. I would be denying this value if I became a hermit, or if I began to act as if there was something more important than being the best human being I can be.

Mary Beth

One of the ways Mary Beth considers that she's acting out her values is by pursuing a creative career in spite of her parents' reservations. But she's as interested in personal wealth as they are. Going back to school for a design degree is a way to live her values, because she believes her degree will translate into money in an artistic field. She convinced her parents to support her in this, and feels lucky she could afford an educational detour. We spoke about the "material" nature of some of her values, as opposed to more "spiritual" values, and she said this: "People don't have a problem if you show you have a strong 'work ethic.' But they do sometimes raise an eyebrow at a very ambitious person like myself. I'm totally driven at the moment. This probably has a lot to do with why I don't have a relationship now, although I yearn to meet my soulmate. But the time is *now* for my career. And I believe it will return me something nearly as nourishing as romantic love. The benefits to my self-esteem, the sense of personal security. And I really deeply believe my success will make me a more evolved person for the one I'll share my life with down the road."

Do you have any doubt that Mary Beth is going to succeed? I don't either.

How might Mary Beth act in a way that goes against her values? She could squander her money. She could take it to Vegas and join a high-stakes poker game, or take up commodity trading at night. She could be irresponsible toward her career, not show up for appointments, give less than 100 percent. She could be untrue to herself and follow her parents' idea of the "right path" instead of her own.

What Gets You Out of Bed in the Morning?

What really makes you happy? What do you *love* to do? Who you are can be inferred from the things that interest you most. These may overlap with some of your values. For instance, Mary Beth values courage, and these are the things she identifies as her passions: skiing, windsurfing, and rock climbing are among them.

I think of values as having more *inner* significance, and passions as being more "of the world." For instance, one of my passions is cooking, which I can't claim to be something I value as much as I value love, but cooking does say something about my desire to nurture the people I love, and is therefore a valuable clue to who I am.

Something else I'm passionate about is television. I have been since I was a little girl. When I was five years old we had a fire at our house, and I made my mother run back inside to save my little white portable Sony TV. I didn't have a favorite doll that I lavished love on. I adored my Sony instead.

Suze Orman, who wrote *9 Steps to Financial Freedom,* tells a poignant story about a death-defying act that taught her the importance of money more vividly than any lesson. She was also a small child when her father's store caught fire, and he ran into his burning building to save the cash register, and carried it out, burning hot, in his bare arms. My devotion to my TV and its importance in my life felt like that.

Our house burned to the ground in our fire, and not very long after that my mom left us and my sister and I became latchkey kids. Until our dad came home from work at night, it was pretty much the TV that kept us company. I tuned in to laugh, learn, and feel safe.

A million events, as big as a house fire, as small as a latchkey, go into forming who we are and what's important to us.

Make a record of those things you love most. It doesn't matter how many items you list. I know some people who are curious and involved in so many different things, it amazes me. I know a woman who's an avid tennis player, who maintains an incredible garden, practices the flute religiously, is dedicated to learning French, loves to travel, and loves water sports of all kinds. But there are also people who have one grand passion only. What matters for our purposes is what those interests are and what they say about you. Someone who lists money, car, clothes, and prestige among her top ten "passions" is a very different brand than the person who lists volunteerism, landscape painting, and meditation.

A different brand. Not a lesser brand, or a superior one. Just different.

These exercises are not about changing who you are. They are about becoming self-aware and about being honest with yourself. They require no judgments, just observation. But if you don't like what you see, it's within your power to make changes.

Branding gives you the opportunity
to become brand-new.

Building the bridge from who you are now to the authentic you is a process that begins deep inside. Although your bridge may soar across a great span, it's the foundation work you do that will guarantee stability and success.

Of all the things you might succeed at, those things you're passionate about give you the best possible chance for success. And yet it's not unusual for people to struggle in some kind of job for which they have no passion, and which doesn't in any way reflect or complement their personal values.

How many people do you know who began their working life by taking the first job offered, without considering if it matched their values and passions? It's not uncommon when you're just starting out. But how many people continue to approach job starts or job changes with a similar sort of indiscriminate "I'll take anything" attitude?

More than you'd think.

In creating a successful brand for your work life, aim to incorporate both your values and your passions in what you do. I've worked hard to create a direct relationship between what I love and what I do in my working life. I think my passion for TV almost guaranteed my success at Turner Broadcasting.

There may be many less obvious relationships, though, between your work and some of your passions. Like cooking, for example. I know a lot of women who get a great deal of pleasure from the whole process of preparing a nice dinner—planning the menu, shopping, cooking, laying the table, and presenting a beautiful and nutritious meal for people they love. I have a lot of the same pleasures doing my work as a brand strategist, cooking up promotional campaigns, coordinating resources almost the way you combine ingredients, laying out artwork, and ultimately presenting something that could definitely be called delicious to my clients.

Are there any common threads among the words you can list as your passions? Do *any* of your passions exist in your present work or in work you're considering moving into? Shouldn't they?

Maybe you think the idea of earning your living doing something you love is a luxury. Maybe you don't believe you could ever be so lucky. I'm here to tell you that "luck" has less to do with making your dreams come true than you think. Conscious, focused effort is way more dependable than luck in achieving goals. But more about this in the next chapter.

What Do You Bring to the Table?

In addition to values and passions, your talents and skills are also an important part of your brand's distinguishing features. So ask yourself what you are really good at. Don't limit yourself to qualities that only seem career-related.

My talents are all about performing: singing, dancing, acting. I have a friend who's a talented pianist and one who's a wonderful painter. I know a woman who can walk into a room where everybody is cranky and at odds, and leave it with everybody smiling and hugs all around. I don't know how she does it, but it's her talent.

Aside from a natural athleticism and a risk-taking nature, Mary Beth is one of those people who can imagine anything and draw it right out of her head. She has a built-in sense of perspective and design that was obvious from her childhood and was encouraged by her family—up to a point. In her teens, when Mary Beth talked about majoring in fine arts in college, her mother told her firmly, "There's nothing attractive about a starving artist."

By the time we're adults, most of us know a few things we do well. But we may be overlooking talents that have fallen by the wayside. Think back to when you were a kid. What did your parents or teachers praise you for? What were your favorite subjects in school? What extracurricular activities did you like best after school?

Sadly, much of our best information about our evolving natural talents ends with childhood and the monitoring and feedback of parents and teachers. That's why it's extremely important to establish a kind of focus group consisting of your most trusted girlfriends or family members. Think of them as your brand advisers. Companies use focus groups all the time to find out how the public perceives their brands. When it comes to brand people, the focus group is at least as important. Because these are your friends and they know you and where you're coming from, unlike less involved, more remote focus groups that corporations hire, you can expect much more relevant feedback. Ask them to tell you what each of them thinks is *your foremost talent.* When you've consulted with them, *write down what they tell you.*

This is valuable brand information that usually reveals something deeper than the skills you may already be aware of. ***This information could be more valuable to your success than an MBA.*** Next ask your focus group to look over the list of work-related attributes I've listed below. If you can count any of these among your talents you may want to emphasize them in your brand description:

Attributes Prized in the Workplace

accomplishment	accountability	ambition
analytical	assertiveness	cheerfulness
competence	competitiveness	cooperation
creativity	decisiveness	dedication
dependability	initiative	determination
eagerness	efficiency	enthusiasm
extroversion	flexibility	good attitude
follow-through	good listener	good-natured
helpfulness	interest	knowledgeable
loyalty	motivation	organization
patience	professionalism	speed
quick thinking	receptivity	reliability
responsibility	economy	skill
smarts	strategist	strength
structure	team playing	thoughtfulness
versatility	eloquence	responsiveness
accessibility	honesty	evenhandedness
inventiveness	perspective	good communicator
visionary	intelligence	energy
commitment	integrity	risk taking

Business Is a Talent Show

In business, these attributes are as much an expression of talent as an ability to play the violin. They are distinguishing characteristics prized by employers, potential clients, the public in general, no matter what the field. They may be counted among your "key attributes," part of the distinguishing characteristics of your brand.

As with other natural talents—your ability to draw, your facility for math or science—if you're a "natural" in any of these areas, you might not even be aware you are distinguished by them. That's where the focus group comes in. You might not consider yourself especially dedicated, but then come to find out that people think your dedication to a project is above and beyond anybody else's. If you adjust easily to a change in circumstances, say a merger or a new boss, you'd be selling yourself short to think you're not more flexible than the next guy.

Using the list above to prompt you, adding those words that speak of your unique brand qualities—your values, your passions, your special skills—*make a record of five key attributes that you want to accentuate for your audience,* whether that audience is your boss or your colleagues at work, or a prospective employer, or your own clients.

In addition to the talents we know we have and the ones other people assure us we have, I believe we also have aptitudes and capabilities that haven't yet been noticed by others or by us. One of the ways we can uncover these is by trying new things. I don't mean quit your day job to experiment. But if you always have a tune running through your head, and you automatically separate out the different instruments when you're listening to a band, but you've never considered that you might have a musical talent, why not pick up an instrument and see what happens?

And when you discover what resonates with your soul, trust it. Although he was an accomplished musician, Sting used to work as a schoolteacher. When he finally sat down and let the music pour through him, "Roxanne" was born, and the rest is music history. The process is more than just finding your talents—you have to honor your talents, too.

At the first of every year, I make a list of what I want to learn or accomplish. Last year painting and boxing were on my list, among other things, and I took a wonderful painting workshop in Big Sur. I turned out to be a less than brilliant painter, but it opened me to my creative self in a way I'd never experienced before and I loved it. I took boxing lessons, too, and that was also great. I came away feeling really strong and self-confident. Both of these experiences were good for my brand because they were so good for me. To help you uncover your hidden talents, I recommend trying two or three new things a year.

Aspire to Become a Specialist

What you call your specialty is of major importance to your brand's success in the workplace. The specialist always makes more money than the general practitioner—it almost doesn't matter what the specialty is. If your goal is to become clearly defined in who you are so you can attract the customer or client or audience you want, one way to succeed is to become a specialist. *Being a generalist is very old news.*

Cable TV is all about specializing. There's the Food Network, The History Channel, Discovery Channel, ESPN, and Comedy Central. There are shopping channels, religion channels, women's channels like Lifetime, and kids-only like Nickelodeon. The broadcast networks that appeal to the masses are beginning to get it that they have to somehow differentiate themselves, too.

It's the same in my "category" as a brand strategist. There are a lot of brand strategists out there, but by specializing in television I've created a niche that's attracted top clients and commanded superior fees.

We assume someone who's gotten her MBA has fundamental business skills, but what's more important is her particular area of expertise. Doctors specialize as oncologists, pediatricians, psychiatrists. Lawyers come in a variety of flavors: personal injury, criminal, patent, corporate. Teachers specialize by subject and grade. Someone who has spent years gardening has probably also developed specialized knowledge, maybe about growing vegetables, planting bulbs, or pruning trees; and so has someone who has practiced a sport, or mastered a game, or read extensively on any particular subject. Some people say that if you read seven books on any one subject, you're an expert.

Mary Beth

For Mary Beth, zeroing in on a specialty was difficult because her talents qualified her in many different areas. She had minored in art in college, studying folk art and design. But her parents had pushed her to major in communications, and she just assumed she'd pursue advertising or marketing. At Parsons she fell in love with the possibilities the Internet held for artists. Now she was thinking that Web design might be the folk art of the twenty-first century.

And then at a Fourth of July party that looked like a *New Yorker* cartoon set in the Hamptons, Mary Beth met Jim, a screenwriter from Hollywood who worked with one of the big studios. The conversation got around to her job search. "Come to L.A.," he said.

The digital age had dawned in Hollywood. It was boom time for the techno-hip who could build and design Web sites and create content. He'd introduce her to some people in his industry. She'd make twice as much money in L.A. as she could make at Grey, he assured her.

Mary Beth was very interested. The idea of relocating to the left coast seemed exciting and adventurous. She could seek her fortune in California, she could become a star in a galaxy of her own construction. There were probably thousands of Web designers in Los Angeles, but how many who worked *exclusively* within the entertainment industry?

Your area of expertise—your specialty—doesn't have to be an art or science. It may be a factor of your personality or one of the prized attributes we've already identified. You might be someone who develops a reputation as a skilled listener. You might be an expert at office politics; or a screenwriter specializing in romantic comedy or science fiction; or you could be someone specializing in consumer research who knows and understands the Internet. From those values, passions, and talents you possess that have money-making potential, narrow your focus to an area that you can develop as your niche or specialty.

Just Do It! Create a Tagline

We all have this in common: We are each one of a kind. There's no one else just like you, with your way of looking at things, with your sense of humor, with your set of values and passions, with your patience or your level of concentration, with your attention to detail or your ability to see the big picture. Unless you're a twin, nobody looks exactly like you. No one puts together words exactly like you do. No one has the same tastes, the same take on things, no one has experienced what you have from where you stand. No one is evolving just like you are.

It's that incredible mix of everything that makes you absolutely unique, and that same magical combination that makes your brand unlike any other.

Your brand is like your thumbprint,
something absolutely, individually yours.

When you've identified your particular skills and best qualities, and accumulated a list of descriptive words and phrases that correspond to your professional self, when you've recognized what makes you one-of-a-kind, and chosen a specialty, you have, in effect, your brand's raw definition. At the end of this chapter, I'll ask you to write out that definition.

It should be one you can live up to day in and day out. Projecting yourself as a super intellect if you aren't one, even though you wish you were, just isn't cool. If I wanted to impress people with how tough I am, I'd never pull it off. Or if I did, it would be pretty exhausting to keep up the act for very long.

People who put up a front at work, or act phony, are usually insecure about their business skills or talent. *There's a fine line between arrogance and confidence, and that line is called fear.* You may get away with faking it for a while, but you can't sustain a phony brand long-term. Ultimately, someone sees through it and then your credibility is blown.

When you think of how to describe your brand, look for something you can deliver consistently. If what you put out there is truly you, this won't be a problem. Your description may be a paragraph long—a lot of material for people to remember when they hear your name: Robin Fisher Roffer. Oh, yeah, she's the one who loves TV, cares most for integrity, empowerment, and love, is motivated and smart, loves to cook, sings and dances, is upbeat, enthusiastic, and on and on and on.

Edit your definition down to a soundbite by hooking it to your job or career in a tagline, a kind of capsule description, the verbal equivalent of a logo that will come to people's minds when they hear your name.

Just to put you in the mood to create your own, here are some brands you may know, and their taglines:

ALLSTATE: "You're in good hands with Allstate"

MAXWELL HOUSE COFFEE: "Good to the last drop"

QUAKER OATS: "Warms your heart and soul"

DEBEERS: "Diamonds are forever"

REVLON: "Products for revolutionary women"

APPLE: "Think different"

HOME DEPOT: "Low prices are just the beginning"

BMW: "The ultimate driving machine"

PREFERENCE BY L'ORÉAL: "Because I'm worth it"

FEDERAL EXPRESS: "The world, on time"

JAGUAR: "A Jaguar is a copy of nothing"

HBO: "It's not TV. It's HBO"

PEPPERIDGE FARM CHOCOLATE CHUNK COOKIE CLASSICS: "Satisfaction is just one bite away"

TLC (THE LEARNING CHANNEL): "Adventures for your mind"

TRAVELOCITY.COM: "Travel virtually anywhere"

JOHN DEERE: "Nothing Runs like a Deere"

AVIS: "We try harder"

LEXUS: "The relentless pursuit of perfection"

NIKE: "Just do it"

Taglines are benefit-driven, aspirational, or descriptive. They say what the consumer will get from the product, or what the product hopes for, or they seek to simply define the product. Home Depot's tagline is clearly benefit-driven. It wants its consumers to know they'll get low prices and lots more. Lexus's "Pursuit of perfection" and Nike's "Just do it" are aspirational, which is a word that combines ambition and desire. John Deere's tagline is purely descriptive (and punny), and so is TLC's—the network features shows that educate and entertain.

Sometimes a tagline qualifies in more than one category. BMW's is all three: aspirational, descriptive, and benefit-driven.

Also notice how these descriptions, which send a powerful message about their products, are all very simple and very positive statements that use words that sell. BMW is the "ultimate," Revlon is "revolutionary," Cookie Classics promise "satisfaction," Lexus aims for "perfection."

The personal tagline you use to sell yourself should also be simple and positive. It should be benefit-driven, aspirational, or descriptive, or a combination of the three. The shorter the tagline, the better.

Remember the brand-name product you personalized for yourself earlier in the chapter. This time, instead of describing yourself as a personality, describe yourself as a professional. Your tagline should be a clear, concise declaration of who you are and what you do.

I have a friend who's an "eco-journalist," another who's a "book doctor," and one who's an Internet content-writer who calls herself a "digital storyteller." I know a personal coach who uses "I'm money in the bank," a librarian at CNN who refers to herself as the "Information Goddess of popular culture," a computer consultant who calls herself a "cybertherapist."

Mary Beth

Mary Beth's *full description* of herself in branding terms reads as follows:

> I'm accountable, motivated, and determined, and a highly creative self-starter. My enthusiasm for adventure and art—from the folk art of West Africa to the newest digital art—provides a worldly, fresh approach to my design sense.

She whittled that description down to this tagline:
Creative Design for Courageous Content

It's a great tag for her, perfectly descriptive, highlighting some of her key benefits and attributes. It says: I'm creative. I'm a designer. I meet courage with courage.

Though it's short, the tagline contains much. It's descriptive, focusing on who Mary Beth is and what she does. It might also have focused on her market niche or specialty, but it doesn't have to. Mary Beth will go after the entertainment industry, but her tagline need not limit her there.

My own tagline is "Brand strategist for the digital age." I use it in all my promotional pieces. At conferences I'm introduced with those words. It's a lot better than "Sweepstakes Queen," I can tell you that. My tagline is descriptive and aspirational. It communicates my interest and my connection with cutting edge media. It accentuates my talent for strategic thinking, which is a positive professional trait and one of my key attributes. It speaks of a whole new industry that really is revolutionizing the world, and puts me among those who are shaping that world.

In creating your tagline, be as specific as you are succinct. I specify "digital age" because branding is happening in every category and my interest leans toward television and the Internet, both very much connected to the digital world. So don't say "Ann Chambers, Creative Marketing." Make it more specific. Say "Ann Chambers, Inventive promotion for inventive products." Don't brand yourself an editorial service; call yourself a Book Doctor, as Carol Costello does, and feature your multiple specialties: "First Aid (editing for style and clarity); Outpatient Procedures (serious rewriting); Major Surgery (deep restructuring)."

Do some detective work to find out how your colleagues at work and other professionals in your field refer to themselves so that you can differentiate yourself. Then think about your values and passions and talents. Your tagline may take inspiration there. But specifically try to *incorporate some of your key benefits or attributes* in the line, *in words that will set you apart.* Your challenge is to capture the essence of what you have to offer, create interest and enthusiasm for it, and enhance your image in the business world.

Take plenty of time developing this important word picture for yourself. How will it look as a kind of caption for your name? How will you feel about being referred to and remembered this way? Although companies do change their taglines as their brands evolve, their intention, and ours, is for the line to last at least for the near long-term. Consider a phrase you can live comfortably with and grow with and you'll always have a quick, focused response to that burning question, "What do you do?"

Step 1 Exercises:
Developing Your Brand Description

1. YOU ARE A PRODUCT: WHAT ARE YOU, AND WHY?

Make a record of the brand you've chosen, and your justification:

I'm _____ because _____
     my brand   *my justification*

Now substitute your name for the brand product you chose, and read the justification as a description:

I'm _____.   I'm _____.

2. IDENTIFY YOUR CORE VALUES.

- Record your three or four core values:

- How do I act out any of these values every day?

- How do I act contrary to my values?

3. IDENTIFY YOUR PASSIONS.

Record those things you're passionate about:

4. IDENTIFY YOUR TALENTS.

- What did your parents praise you for?

- What were your favorite subjects in school?

- What activities did you like best after school?

- What do you consider your talents?

(CONTINUES)

- What do others see as your talents?

- Three new things you might like to try over the next six months:

5. WHAT ARE YOUR FIVE KEY TALENTS OR ATTRIBUTES?

6. WHAT WILL YOU DEVELOP AS YOUR SPECIALTY?

7. WRITE YOUR BRAND DESCRIPTION.

It should contain the intentions of your core values, passions, and natural talents; it should express your key attributes. It can emphasize your specialty.

8. IDENTIFY YOUR BRAND WITH A TAGLINE.

Boil down your brand description into one succinct line that's descriptive, aspirational and/or benefit driven.

Define Your Dreams and Put Them into Action

I haven't read every self-help book ever written, but I'd guess that most of them, no matter what the subject, contain a chapter somewhere up near the front that's all about objectives (also known as dreams, goals, and aspirations). This is because, as Yogi Berra once said, "If you don't know where you're going, you'll end up somewhere else." Clearly imagined goals, down to their finest details, are essential to the entire process of becoming successful. *Every respected brand has very specific objectives.*

Let's talk for a second about what it means for a brand to be a "success." Of course it will vary brand to brand, as it does person to person, but very basically a successful brand satisfies two masters. The brand's company or corporation is one master, the brand's customers are the other. Frosted Flakes must serve the Kellogg Corporation, as well as the people who eat sugar-coated cornflakes. Ford's Explorer is expected to be profitable for the Ford Motor Company, and it also has to meet its buyers' expectations for performance and durability.

When you apply brand strategies to yourself in your career,

you're focusing on the benefits you provide your employer, or if you're self-employed, your clients. This is the equivalent of meeting your customers' expectations. It's also important to identify the benefits you want for yourself. As your own sole proprietor, how do *you* intend to profit from your brand?

Goals Come in All Sizes

It's crucial to be specific about your goals, and to record them in a way that's measurable, so you can evaluate how effectively your brand strategy is working year to year. Your goal might be to earn $100,000 this year, or to get three choice projects handed to you, or be promoted to vice president or upper management, or to earn an industry award or mention in a trade journal. In some professions success is measured in prestige or tenure rather than dollars. Your brand objective of the moment might be to get published, or be invited to a particular conference. Or you could be focused on attracting a valuable client ("gaining market share"), or a government grant, or on renewing an important contract.

Companies frequently hire marketing experts and brand strategists to create awareness in a specific market or within a certain demographic. Your brand goal might be exactly the same—to get noticed—or maybe your objective is to break out on your own. This was the case for Jillian.

Jillian

She and her husband both work hard to sustain their comfortable lifestyle. He's a prize–winning author, she's been a bookkeeper for the past thirteen years. They own their own home in a very desirable northern California location.

Jillian is the major contributor to the family income, managing five popular eating places for a single female powerhouse in the resort community where they live. When Jillian came to see me, she was looking for change. She was tired of being an employee, tired of feeling limited by her salary. She was fifty-one and felt an urgency about getting proactive. She wanted to grab some control over her future.

And so her immediate goal became to strike out on her own, to become one of the 10 to 12 million other women working independently in the United States. She would offer similar financial services to those she provided her restaurateur, both planning and management, and she'd aim her services at other small-to-medium sized businesses in her coastal town.

Following the same process you went through in the previous chapter, Jillian defined her **key attributes** and formed a **brand description:**

Jillian's Key Attributes:

- One-stop shopping for business support

- Detail-oriented, accurate, professional

- Acts like the surrogate CFO

- Excellent references, track record of success

- Familiar with Quick Books Pro and Multi Ledger

Jillian's Brand Description

Small business owners turn to Jillian for everything from bookkeeping to insurance and retirement programs, and advice on employee issues. A manager to depend on for all financial matters, Jillian is an indispensable asset whose vast experience and resources create an efficient and effective back office for busy entrepreneurs.

Jillian's Tagline

Financial solutions for small businesses

Big Brands = Big Money

When I help a client brand a Web site or television network, I expect and my client expects that the results will have a direct positive impact on the brand's long-term economic situation. When a company asks itself, "What are our objectives?" one obvious answer is: "To increase bottom line." E-Toys wants to make a lot of money. So does The Gap. So does Campbell's Soup. So do the Fox Network and Procter & Gamble.

When I think of myself as my own brand manager, I also expect that my personal success will be reflected in financial success. Most of us who work want to make enough money to live well and retire well. But understanding what "living well" means and predicting what "retiring well" will require may be some of life's greatest challenges. For many women, for many years, these were irrelevant questions. Someone else was going to take care of all that. Today they are primary motivators for our careers.

Nail Down Your Financial Goals

What do you need to make a living? What do you dare aspire to? Companies all have a dollar amount that their brands must earn, but they're also always reaching out to do better, to do more. To start, research the standard salary range for the position you're aiming for and know how far you can go from where you're starting. You can get this information from trade organizations within your target industry, and salary surveys for many different kinds of professions can be found on the Web. Check out jobstar.org, for example, or salary.com. There are many others.

Mary Beth

Investigating standard salaries, Mary Beth concluded that Jim's "You'll make twice as much," was an exaggeration. She called several friends from grad school who were working in the digital world, and did an informal survey. Website builders were swarming to California. Ordinarily that kind of competition kept salaries down. But Mary Beth wasn't afraid of competition. She loved challenge. She was in a no-fear zone when it came to what she wanted. And she thought "twice as much" might actually be within her grasp if she made herself into a successful brand.

If you're starting your own business, what do comparable businesses make in your location? If you're a freelancer, what are others in your field charging for similar services?

Jillian

Jillian would like to bring in $40,000–$50,000 a year. Though she's their main source of income, their low mortgage and Philip's occasional windfalls make Jillian feel as if that amount would be "enough," allowing for a little travel, a few extras without the guilt, and maybe leaving something left over for retirement savings. I encouraged her to aim higher.

We agreed she'd dare to think in terms of earning $60,000–$70,000 a year.

Now it became a matter of fairly simple mathematics to figure out how many clients a year at what retainer per month Jillian would need to accomplish her goal.

But she had been out of competition for a long time. She wasn't up on what other industries paid for the kinds of services she could offer, so she opened the Yellow Pages, found phone numbers for a representative group of financial assistants, bookkeepers, tax consultants, and planners, and called them.

This isn't proprietary information. Anyone can ask. In a short time, Jillian had had a number of very informative conversations and learned that she could charge anywhere from $1,000 to $2,000 a month for various combinations of services.

Although we represent 49 percent of the workforce, figuring out what to charge is a lot harder for women than for men. Instead of being a measure of the value of our work and key benefits, fees and salaries get all tangled up with questions of self-worth—and I have to tell you, this is a problem for a lot of women.

It doesn't help that as a sex we're paid considerably less than men. In the cable industry, on average, women get 15 percent less than men in the same jobs doing the same work with the same degree of excellence—and that's a lot better than women in other industries. According to the Bureau of Labor Statistics, women generally earn 23 percent less than men doing the same work. What does that say about how we're valued?

Also complicating our relationship with money, many women in the workforce grew up in homes where the Prince Charming myth was still popular. They never really believed that their career would be more than a stopgap before marriage, and marriage meant that someone else would be the breadwinner. They never developed a sense of their personal financial potential, or even of themselves as self-sufficient.

This was never my problem. I always knew I could take care of myself—because I *had* to take care of myself as a child, and because my dad never suggested there were any limits to how far I could go in business.

I may have been the original "take your daughter to work" kid. My dad was an advertising executive. He took me along with him when he pitched a client, and he taught me how to lay out ads and write copy. He guided me into advertising with expert hands. There was never a question what my path would be in life.

But I've still had a lot of personal issues with money because for a time when I was very young I lived in extremely impoverished circumstances. It made me absolutely sure I never wanted to go there again. In a way it gave me my first life goal: to never be poor, to always have enough—to have more than enough—to keep a reserve, a safety net. Even today, though I'm successful by anyone's standards, I'm careful to save fifty cents out of every dollar I make.

I probably still have issues about money. I would say most women do—but we're making progress. I've found that when we think of ourselves as "brands" and work at increasing our product value in the workplace, it practically guarantees a major boost to self-esteem because it's such a positive, proactive process, and because it gets results. And you can measure the results. Having said that, we still have to work harder and better than the boys to make their same salaries. It's like what ex-Texas governor Ann Richards said about Ginger Rogers and Fred Astaire: She did exactly what he did, only she had to do it in high heels, and backwards.

What Are You Really Worth?

Experience teaches us something about what to ask, but it's so much more efficient to talk to other people in your field to develop a sense of what's too much and what's too little and what's worth trading dollars for. Networking here is really critical, and not so different from how a company figures out what price to put on its brand product. First they survey all the other products in their brand's category. Then they position themselves in relation to those other products. Some brands price themselves lower than the competition to attract a bigger customer base; others make themselves very expensive and are promoted as top-of-the-line.

Much of the cachet of driving a Mercedes-Benz has to do with its high price. Not just anyone can afford one. That's part of its brand appeal. You still think "expensive" when you think Mercedes, even though the company has begun producing less expensive cars. In the long run, this may prove detrimental. It's true that Mercedes has broadened its customer base by manufacturing a less pricey product, but the fact that it's more accessible to more people now may ultimately damage its brand identity, which was all about exclusivity. Time will tell.

Customers believe they're getting the best when they pay the most, and the same is true of your customers. But you'd better not disappoint them. Remember how important authenticity and consistency are to your brand's success. Don't pretend to be the best in your field unless you're sure you are. Don't charge more for your services or ask for a salary in excess of industry averages unless you offer "value-added" benefits, more than the standard product or service, and can demonstrate it by being consistently more competent, more reliable, more flexible, quicker—whatever your claim is. The Infiniti offers its customers roadside assistance, courtesy pickup, and loaner cars, and charges more than other cars in its mid-range category, at the same time it distinguishes itself from its competition. Nordstrom is a department store not a whole lot different than others, but it offers a "personal shopper" service, and will charge customers something extra for that distinguishing characteristic.

On the other hand, except at the very beginning of your career when you might accept a lower salary or lower fee or commission than you'd like in order to get in the door, don't charge less for your work than you're worth. And except for *extraordinary* circumstances, which you'll have to judge for yourself, *never* give it away. It's a psychological truth that work that's given away is not valued by the recipient. So trade your services, or arrange a payment plan, or extend credit, or agree to a low starting salary with an automatic raise after three months, but don't do it for nothing. You'll never do yourself a favor by putting your brand value at zero.

My friend Lucane taught me this. She's from Ireland, and came to this country with a desire to do event marketing. She didn't have a whole lot of experience, and so when the agency she was interviewing with asked her to do an event plan for a software company as a kind of audition—gratis—she didn't feel she was in a position to refuse. If they liked her proposal, they told her, they'd let her execute it for a fee.

You can guess the outcome. She put hours of effort into the project, submitted it with great expectations, and never heard from them again. Welcome to America.

On the other hand, when Mary Beth decided to pursue Jim's

connection with a start-up Web design company, she spent some time doing an evaluation of their current Web site, turning in a thoughtful, three-page document the week before her scheduled interview. This is what she told me:

> I don't believe in giving it away. I actually considered the time I spent on my analysis to be prep time for the interview. It told me a lot more than I would have known otherwise. For one thing it really affirmed for me that I wanted to work for them. Also it gave me a lot to talk about in the interview. I had ideas for them, I was focused and informed.

Of course you take a risk doing something for nothing, but if you do it for your own benefit, like Mary Beth did, that's a very different thing than doing it as a benefit for a would-be employer who has everything to gain (your ideas, your time and effort) and nothing to lose, while the opposite can be said for you.

Living the Good Life

Understanding what "living well" means is another evolutionary process. In the sixties, when my sister and I were five and six years old and living poor in L.A., I probably would have defined living well as having enough to eat. In the seventies "living well" was how we lived with my dad in Cleveland, whose orderly, middle-class life made us feel safe after years of scary uncertainty.

Today my standards for living well still have to do with safety, but they also have to do with adventure and with beautiful things. I love to travel. I feel good about spending my money on new experiences and making memories. Living well, for me, has to do with being able to buy time: To afford someone to come in and clean my house once a week. To hire an assistant who will run errands, make copies, and handle the phones.

What will it take for you to live the way you want to live? How *do* you want to live? In the country or the city? Married or single? Be very specific here. You know the adage, "Be careful what you wish for—you may just get it!"

In fact, you're very likely to get what you ask for, because when you finally uncover and get serious about your heart's desire, the universe starts listening.

So if you ask for a home in the country, for instance, be sure to specify if a fixer-upper is what you had in mind. If you ask for the love of a man in your life, don't forget to specify an *unmarried* man. Or if you ask for celebrity status, be prepared for mob scenes and a lot of hype and the end of life as you've known it—or ask for celebrity *and* privacy.

What does living well mean to you? I'm talking materially, but not *only* about material things. Living well is being well, and being happy, and enjoying life. Most people would agree that these goals are even more important than the monetary ones. Fortunately, we don't have to choose between them—we can have them both. When we're *really* successful, our life goals and money goals complement one another.

Living the passions and values that you identified for your brand description in the previous chapter is what living well will be all about for you.

Jillian

Jillian defined her passions as her home and garden, beautiful clothes, and music. The most important things to her, she said, were harmony, balance, and equanimity—the kind of peace she experiences working in her garden. For Jillian living well is living in harmony—with work and home, with her husband, with her mother—and without feeling stressed over money.

Mary Beth

> Mary Beth's idea of living well is "to have a condo in Aspen and a bungalow in the Hollywood Hills where I can telecommute a couple of days a week."

For those of us who are forging new and exciting paths career-wise, living well has much to do with working well. Working in an environment or situation that suits your personality or your personal style is important and should count high among those things you aim for. Look at the following list to decide which statements apply most to you. Use these as a starting-off point. Add more specifics. You're trying to visualize the ideal situation for you.

Personality/style-based preferences

I'd like to work for a big corporation.

I prefer to work at home.

I want to retire at age forty-five.

I don't ever want to retire from work I love.

I'd like to work in a creative field.

I prefer a more structured environment.

I want to work with people like myself.

I want to work with people who are different from me.

I like my work to be a challenge.

I like work that I can do without even thinking.

I enjoy working under pressure.

I can't stand deadlines.

I want to be my own boss.

I'd like to travel.

I want flexible hours.

I don't want a long commute.

You'd be amazed at how few people think about what they want and don't want when they consider their working life. This is because most people don't think they can have what they want, and some people feel lucky to be working at any job at all. That's why I recommend creating a wish list for your work life that encompasses personal preferences—those things that will make you happiest.

My friend Kim Youngblood, president and creative strategist at Youngblood, Sweat & Tears, knew she had achieved a certain measure of success when her professional circumstances allowed her to (1) bring her dog to work, (2) open her office windows for fresh air in springtime, and (3) not have to wear pantyhose or high heels.

Jillian

Jillian knew she didn't want to work in an office behind a restaurant any more. She preferred a structured work environment, but was highly disciplined and knew she could create her own structure at home. She was willing to spend time in any of the small businesses she took on as clients, but would convert her guest bedroom into an office for herself that would be a sanctuary, a place of order and calmness conducive to her work.

Mary Beth

Mary Beth had different goals. She wanted people around, she wanted buzz. Jim had suggested she could freelance her services as a Web designer, but her preference was to work in-house for a new Internet start-up or Web-based design firm.

Big and small companies also make preferential decisions. Some places expect you in suit and stockings and a modest stacked heel. There's a certain atmosphere of quiet productivity, and not a lot of gossip around the cappuccino machine. Socializing is not particularly encouraged. I know a big import company in San Francisco that's like that. To work there and be happy you really have to be a certain kind of person.

And then there are companies like House & Gardens TV (HGTV), winner of Women in Cable's Accolades Award. Their family-friendly environment focuses on employee lifestyle concerns, which include flextime, child care referral assistance, even adoption assistance, and community outreach. It doesn't come as too much of a surprise that HGTV's upper management includes fourteen women.

There are Web sites that provide insider information about what it's *really* like to work for specific companies. Check out www.vault-reports.com or www.wetfeet.com, for example.

Dharma and the Mission Statement

In addition to a money objective, every company that stands behind a brand has a "mission," which communicates the brand's soul and its purpose in life. To help companies define their brand's purpose, and to keep it uppermost in corporate consciousness, marketing departments or brand strategists develop company "mission statements" based on a company's objectives for its product.

While the brand's tagline acts as a zippy sound bite that lets consumers know what benefits they'll gain from the product, or what the product is or does, the mission statement acts more like an affirmation and motivational tool for the company and the product's brand manager.

The mission statement expresses the company's highest ideals on behalf of its brand. In these statements we find a deeper-than-money objective; we find the company's values as embodied in its product. When you think of a mission statement, think trumpets in the background; imagine a drum roll.

Companies with powerful mission statements
and employees that embrace these statements
walk the walk and talk the talk.

Whereas a company tries to make its tagline a familiar phrase for the public, the mission statement may or may not be advertised. Eddie Bauer uses its "creed" in its ads, but more often consumers never see or hear of a company's mission statement. It's more important that the company, the brand makers and promoters, know their mission and keep it alive, than for the customer to know about it.

On the other hand, isn't it nice to learn that big corporations have higher goals than their bottom lines? For some examples of mission statements, check out the following:

EDDIE BAUER: "To give you such outstanding quality, value, service and guarantee that we may be worthy of your high esteem."

NIKE: "To lead in corporate citizenship through proactive programs that reflect caring for the world family."

COCA-COLA: "To refresh a thirsty world."

WALT DISNEY: "Using the power of entertainment to educate and enlighten."

MARY KAY COSMETICS: "To provide women with an unparalleled opportunity for financial independence, career, and personal fulfillment."

SONY: "To make dreams come true."

MCDONALD'S: "To be the world's leading food service organization."

IBM: "To provide a networked world that transforms the way people work, interact, learn and do business."

The mission statement wants to be a self-fulfilling prophecy. If Eddie Bauer achieves its goal, the high esteem of its customers will make the company rich. If Nike is a good corporate citizen, you can bet that athletes will want to associate their personal brands with Nike. If McDonald's becomes the world's leading food service organization, it's very likely to be the world's most profitable food service organization.

For individuals, the mission statement pulls us toward our possibilities, our dreams. My friend Kim says they're the verbal equivalent of reaching for the stars.

The mission statement should resonate with your core values and express your higher ideals.

I tell people to try to articulate their mission in seven words or less. It will be easier to remember that way, and you want to be able to think of it easily, like you would a motto, when you need to be reminded of who you are and what you stand for. Kim's mission statement is "To clear space for the highest creativity in myself and others." Mine is "Empowering women to lead more directed lives." If it sounds a little grand, it's supposed to. The personal mission statement comes straight from the heart.

Mia Hamm is the "poster girl for women's soccer," according to the news media, although her teammates have tagged her "the reluctant diva" because she's never sought fame or fortune. Instead, the twenty-seven-year-old World Cup winner has kept her mission in front of her: "To make women's soccer more visible." So far she's doing pretty well. Nike has named a building after her, there's a soccer-playing Barbie called Mia, and she's been on the covers of *Time* and *Newsweek* promoting the sport.

I have a friend who's an attorney whose mission is "To help others achieve their goals." Simple, to the point. These words say what she does, and remind her that she's in service to others. Anna Garcia, whose whole family worked in the steel industry, is president of ANKO Metal Services, Inc., in Denver. Her business maxim is "Steel is not just my business, it's my heritage."[1] It reminds her of the depth of her connection to her work.

When you're feeling down, if you face a career setback, reciting your mission should pick you up and put you back on track.

Mary Beth

Mary Beth constructed this mission statement: "To have profound influence over digital design."

Jillian

Jillian's mission statement, framed above her desk, is "To nurture and grow small businesses."

Create a mission statement for yourself and write it out. *Never underestimate the power of the pen. When you commit your dreams to paper, you release them out into the world.* You take them out of the realm of ideas and move them an inch closer to reality. Now they exist in your mind *and* on the page. Then when you *speak* of your dreams you move them another inch closer to reality. Now they are in your mind and on the page and out in the universe. Now other people can hear them and then they're that much more real. And then when you *act* on your dreams, you move them closest of all to reality.

So begin by printing out your mission statement in some appropriately beautiful calligraphic font and post it where you'll see it frequently. In your office, on your mirror. Spell it out in magnetic words on the refrigerator door. Make it into a screensaver or a mousepad. Carry it as a bookmark. Allow it to become part of your environment. Begin to possess it.

We may not be able to have everything we ask for, and we may not be able to have it all at the same time—but on the other hand, maybe we can. In either case, putting our desires out in the universe is the very first step to fulfilling them.

I have a friend, Gerry Graff, who's a writer. She told me this story about how she got her first computer in 1982.

"Visualization" was a new word to me, but it came with such high recommendations that I thought I'd give it a try. I cut a picture of a computer out of a magazine and pinned it to the wall above my typewriter where I would see it pretty much constantly during the day. Not too much later I began a book project with a fellow. He'd give me his hard copy and I'd rewrite it and hand back a freshly typed chapter. Then he'd retype it in order to have it on a disk so he could work on it, and then when I got it back I had to cut and paste and retype, and so forth. After a couple of months he said, "Wouldn't it be nice if we were both using compatible computers? Then we could just trade disks back and forth." I said, "Yes, wouldn't it be nice." And then he offered to trade me a computer for a month's work. Next thing I knew there was an Apple II sitting under that picture I'd pinned to the wall.

The universe is waiting for you to say what you want.

All you need to do is cooperate—to speak, or write, and then to watch and listen. If what you want is solid, if it's thought through, if it's well-defined, if it satisfies your mission statement, the universe is going to deliver. *Everything that you are seeking is also seeking you.* If you put your goals and dreams out in the world, you'll attract whatever it is you're looking for, whether it's a promotion, or a new client, or a new computer.

Creating a Double Life

In addition to your mission statement, in the exercises at the end of this chapter I'm going to ask you to record *everything you want from your career,* by which I mean all your objectives, and all your dreams.

What do you want financially, what do you want materially? Ask yourself if you're "living well" in the very broadest sense: Are you living up to your expectations? Are you passionate about your life? Or have your expectations changed? Or your passions? What do you want emotionally? How do you want to feel about yourself and your occupation?

What would you really, truly like to be doing with your life? Forget about your career for a minute. What would you *really* like to be doing? Dare to have dreams. And then dare to let them come true—even if it means living a double life like my friend Vivien does.

Vivien Stone was a vice president of marketing at a pay-per-view company in California. She does very well because she's very talented, but her real passion lies in writing and selling plays. Her dream is to see one of her plays produced on a Broadway stage. And she does more than just dream it. She gets up early every day, goes in to work, and from seven to nine every morning, she *is* a playwright. She's been learning and polishing her craft, keeping her dream alive, speaking about it to friends and colleagues, and writing and producing plays in local theaters. She's been *manifesting* her dream.

Vivien could go anywhere in business. She's the best, and like cream she would just naturally rise to the top. But her real true objective is to write for the stage.

Why not give up the nine-to-five routine and go all out for writing? Because she's a single mom whose greatest passion of all is her five-year-old son, and whose personal mission is to provide a safe and nurturing environment for him. So she does her best in business, but she doesn't let her dream diminish. She moves laterally instead of up the ladder at work, and in this way she preserves her priorities.

Recently Vivien moved to New York with her son and took a marketing job with a big Broadway theater that promises to put her in closer contact with a creative community.

There are lots of people leading "double lives" to this degree—who want to sing with a band but have mouths to feed or other responsibilities, so they're a programmer by day and sing in a local club at night. Or they drive a taxi to support the beginnings of an acting career. Or they quietly pursue a course of education at night—all in pursuit of their dreams. They know it's up to them to set their dreams in motion.

Step 2 Exercises:
Defining Your Objectives

1. DEFINE YOUR GOALS

Make them specific:

• to earn $ _____ in _____ years
  (Record standard fees or salary range for your target
  position:)

• to retire at age _____

• to pick up _____ new clients this year, or

• to pick up _____ choice projects

• to get noticed by _____

• to be recognized by receiving _____

2. DEFINE WHAT "LIVING WELL" MEANS FOR YOU.

Let's be real. It's *possible* this is our one and only life. Give
your dreams a chance by writing them down here. They
may not have anything to do with your job. Write them
down anyway. What does living well look like, what does it
contain? Be very specific. Write paragraphs.

_____

_____

_____

Personality-based work preferences make work a pleasure and contribute to living well. Record your work preferences here:

_____

_____

_____

3. CREATE YOUR MISSION STATEMENT.

Compose a short statement that contains what matters most to you, and that reminds you of your purpose, and inspires you. Try to keep it at seven words or less. Record the statement here, then post it prominently in your environment. Make it part of your everyday life.

_____

_____

_____

4. STRATEGIZE HOW TO MAKE YOUR DREAMS COME TRUE.

Will it require living a "double life" (for example, student by night, department manager by day)?

Jot down possible scenarios for promoting your goals even when you're not actively engaging them.

_____

_____

_____

Go After Your Target Audience with a Vengeance

No matter what your brand's mission or your financial goal or your personal dreams, identifying and earning the devotion of your target audience are the interlocking and necessary means to reaching those objectives.

One of the golden rules of brand marketing is to know your audience inside and out. So before any brand is introduced to the public, a very careful **market analysis** is undertaken in order to answer these burning questions:

Who is the target audience?

Where is the target audience?

What do they think about our brand?

What do we want them to think?

How will we attract them to our product?

Who is competing for their loyalty?

How Lifetime Television Identified Its Audience

You may find this hard to believe, but in the early 1990s women's programming beyond soap operas was not considered a viable investment, not by networks, not by sponsors other than the detergent crowd and manufacturers of feminine products. Lifetime was the first network that dared to define their target audience as women—which included women at home and women outside the home and women with interests beyond the soaps.

Where was the audience? She was everywhere, and totally ignored.

Lifetime knew that it wanted women to look at its offering as a godsend: finally, programming that appealed to a world of women's interests!

How to attract the target was almost a no-brainer. Program the network for women and promote the hell out of it. Advertise and women should respond—after all, there was nothing else like Lifetime. So the network began to call itself "television for women," and it put that tagline on everything from their own channel to billboards on the Sunset Strip. In a year's time Lifetime's ratings reflected their success, attracting a large and growing audience. And as soon as the audience was there, sponsors were sure to follow, and as soon as the sponsors were on board, the network was sure to become profitable. And so it went for Lifetime TV.

Until recently Lifetime has had no competition to speak of. They were the first network to decide to fill a void and target women all day and all night long. But they have plenty of competition now. The Food Network and HGTV may not target women specifically, but they do attract a large number. Romance Classics, ABC's SoapNet, and Oxygen, Gerry Laybourne, Marcy Carsey, and Oprah Winfrey's twenty-four-hour-a-day women's channel are driving hard to grab a spot on your cable channel line-up, so it's only a matter of time until Lifetime feels the heat. The choices for Lifetime's audience are constantly expanding, so Lifetime is constantly looking to keep its programming fresh, and at the same time build its brand position and maintain its ratings leadership as *the* #1 television destination for women.

Who Matters Anyway?

When we move brand strategies into the realm of our own careers, we must also ask *who will buy what we have to sell.* For us the audience is the corporate world or, if we are in business for ourselves, our customers. As we're using the word here, the target audience is the buyer.

Knowing your audience is as important as knowing what you've got to sell. To make that point, Pierre Mornell, a hiring consultant for businesses and universities, tells the story of Mickey Searles in his book, *Games Companies Play:*[1]

Know Your Audience

Mickey was a thirty-five-year-old hotshot, president of a chain of department stores, who went to interview with Charles Lazarus, the legendary founder of Toys R Us and Kids R Us. Mickey's goal was to become a top executive in a major department store chain, so he was only slightly interested in a new specialty retailer devoted to children's clothing, even if it was Charles Lazarus.

But the interview was "electric," according to Mickey, until he admitted to Mr. Lazarus that he had never visited a Kids R Us store, and the older man abruptly ended the interview.

Mickey thought he might have blown the opportunity of a lifetime. He wrote to Lazarus saying that if they ever met again, he would know more about the Kids R Us chain than Lazarus himself. Mr. L. took Mickey's persistence and humility as good signs and they did meet again. And this time Mickey came prepared.

He had made a project of learning about Charles Lazarus and his companies. For years to follow, Mickey Searles served as president of Kids R Us.

Make your study of the company or client or culture that you want to become part of, or are a part of, as in-depth as possible. Visit the place you hope to work. Read the literature the company or clients generate themselves, but also research the Internet for other information. Read recent news stories on the subject of your search. *Fortune, Business Week,* and *Fast Company* are must-reads beyond your industry trades.

Know your company's history as well. Learn its values. I always buy stock in my clients' companies so that I can keep up on what's really happening with them through annual reports and quarterly updates.

Mary Beth

Mary Beth will be looking for interesting companies from now on. Her *Wall Street Journal* may turn something up. She'll surf the Web and research client lists of L.A.-based designers. She'll subscribe to *Daily Variety, The Hollywood Reporter, Wired,* and *The Industry Standard.* She'll run a search for news items on the companies she considers possibilities and for financial information about them. She'll call the companies she likes for whatever material they put out about themselves.

And beyond this, before Mary Beth goes in for any job interview, she's going to see if she can find out who she'll be meeting with. Then before she meets him or her she'll try to find out everything she can about that person. She'll find out if possible, the kind of car he drives, where he likes to vacation, favorite restaurants—anything for a sense of who he is. Because in this setting the interviewer is Mary Beth's audience—the one she'll want to sell her brand to. So what are the interviewer's accomplishments? What are his values? Is that why he chose this company? How long has he been with the company? How old is he? If she discovers he's a ski nut, for example, or a rock climber, she'll be able to distinguish herself merely by mentioning that those are some of her passions.

The more you know the more comfortable you're going to feel, the better a connection you'll be able to make, and the better able to pitch yourself at the right key. But don't be unreal. Don't try to be what you're not. If it's a bad fit, it wouldn't have worked out anyway.

I've written target audience definitions for many companies, including my own. You can be as specific as you like, and the more specific the better; and the more areas of interest you target, the better it is. For myself, what follows is exactly who I want my clients to be:

BIG FISH MARKETING'S TARGET AUDIENCE:

Vice presidents and directors of marketing at television networks and technology companies who are:

- seasoned pros

- politically savvy

- open to new ideas

- committed to excellence

- clear about what they want

- supportive of the creative process

You can take it a step further. I've also written up precisely the relationship I want with my clients:

DESIRED RELATIONSHIP WITH AUDIENCE:

Ongoing project work or retainer fee based on growth strategies rather than instant problem solving. Mutual respect is paramount. Decisions are made and committed to. Streamlined approval process and flexibility are key.

And I've thought out and written up the kinds of projects I want to work on:

TARGET PROJECT STATEMENT:

Branding focused, multi-component jobs such as marketing plans, brand manuals, sales support materials, and promotional campaigns that build awareness and revenue for a network, Web site, or technology product.

Be an Evolutionary Brand

If you've been in business for a while, you know that you (and therefore your product) *and* your target audience are very likely to change over time. While brand consistency is key, evolution is almost always part of the life of a long-lived brand.

If a company's product appeals to the Gen-X crowd, that company has got to ask, "Will they still love it when they're forty?" And if not, will the next generation of kids think it's cool, or dorky?

We're talking about staying power, a brand byword. Some brands have it, others don't. The Pet Rock was a flash in the pan. Cabbage Patch dolls came and went. One of our goals is to be around for the long term—like Crayola Crayons.

And so part of maintaining any good brand is a review process, which requires frequent monitors of the product relative to the target audience and even the culture. Crayola Crayons is a great example. In the fifties, Prussian Blue became "Midnight Blue" when teachers complained that kids didn't know where Prussia was. In the sixties, influenced by the civil rights movement, the company changed their "Flesh"-colored crayon to "Peach." Even more recently, in response to customer comments, they changed "Indian Red" to "Chestnut."

The need to stay in touch with what's happening outside of your specialized area of concentration can't be stressed enough. It's easy to bury yourself in your work, making crayons, for instance, and not notice that the world has changed around you. Companies use focus groups in order to assure they stay current with what's up. You can do the same. This is an opportunity to call regular meetings of your trusted group of brand advisers, the family members and friends you talk to about your working life. Their perspective, from outside your box, is totally necessary to the evolution of your brand.

We can't just forget about our customers once we've established who they are. We have to always be looking at our brand and at our audience and asking, "Is this working?" "Have I lost any customers lately?" "Does the client always seem happy to see me or hear from me?" "Have I been passed over for a promotion or a plum project recently?" "Has my staff been cut?" The question is not only "Who is my target audience?" but *"How* is my target audience?—and *what does my audience think or feel about me?"*

Laura

Laura had come to the conclusion that her primary target audience, the major package goods corporation she had worked with for the past four years, didn't think *enough* about her. Laura worked late, she took work home, she took on unreasonable deadlines, she worked weekends, while her kids were growing up missing her company. Her efforts were appreciated, she knew, but her annual salary of $60,000 didn't truly reflect the time or talent she brought to her job. She wanted to change that.

Laura was thirty-five, had been married for thirteen years, and had children ten and twelve years old. They lived quite comfortably in a modest colonial house in the suburbs outside Philadelphia. Most days she and her husband drove into the city together to their respective jobs. Laura is a presentation specialist for her company. She's a multi-media and communications expert, someone who can take your idea or your report, turn it into something visually riveting, and teach you how to deliver that idea or that report in a way that both engages and informs an audience.

She handles the presentation work for the top executives at her company, managing a department of eight and occasional freelance graphics help. Branding should help Laura establish the contribution she makes to building her company's business, and earn her a significant raise.

What Do I Want Them to Think?

The other side of "What does my audience think about me?" is "What do I *want* them to think about me?" Successful branding is about making the answer to both questions coincide, and successful brand strategists think about these questions and commit their answers to paper—the equivalent of putting their desires for the brand out in the universe.

I asked Laura to stand in the shoes of her "audience," those executives she wanted to value her more. What did she want them to say about her? I asked Mary Beth and Jillian to do the same. I told them to make their mock testimonials as positive as they could. We are looking for raves. Here's what they wrote:

Laura's Audience Statement:

Laura is an extremely conscientious, hardworking, quality-minded associate. She's customer-focused and an effective consultant. Most of all, she's an educator who aims for the highest level of communication. Laura makes my material interesting and exciting—even when the subject is as dry as an FDA approval or patents pending. She's a born teacher from whom I'm learning the presentation skills I need to get my point across.

Mary Beth's Audience Statement:

FUTURE EMPLOYER: I need someone who really knows what it means to show up for work. I find a lot of twenty-somethings careless and arrogant. Mary Beth is a breath of fresh air. She gets the job done while elevating my firm's creative capabilities to new heights.

FUTURE CLIENTS: Innovative design has been the cornerstone of my brand. I need someone who can take the look and feel I've established to the next level in a digital format. Mary Beth's the one I can turn to. She's a creative risk-taker with a real head for business!

Jillian's Audience Statement:

My books are a real challenge. I'm trying to run a business. I don't have time to deal with payroll, invoices, and receivables. With Jillian, my problems are solved. She handles clients and vendors with diplomacy and care. I trust her completely. She's a whiz with my books, and I can turn to her with any business problem and count on her total discretion and her best efforts.

Before you try to appeal to your audience,
do a 180-degree turn and stand in their shoes.

In the exercise section at the end of this chapter, I've asked you to pretend you are your audience. Ask yourself what you'd like that audience to think about you. Or before you make your presentation before the department heads, imagine you are one of the people receiving the presentation. You might write:

> Impressive. She really put a lot of work into that report. It's clear she has a talent for coordinating a lot of other people's input. And I never realized how well-spoken she is. I could sure use someone like that in *my* department. Maybe I could tempt her with a better salary than what she's getting now.

Once again, you're telling the universe what you want—committing your intentions and your dreams to paper. Making them suddenly more than an idea. Making them more solid, something you can *see*. Taking them giant steps closer to reality.

How Am I Doing?

Nickelodeon, one of the highest rated cable networks, and one of the three most profitable networks in TV history, is all about "putting kids first and being kids-focused." As it has grown, Nickelodeon has conducted hundreds of focus groups, and taken major surveys on what kids like and don't like, what they care about, and what concerns them. Nickelodeon knows exactly how kids feel about its network because it asks them at every opportunity and then shapes itself in order to provide precisely what they want. In spite of growing competition from other children's TV programming, Nickelodeon maintains its brand status as the best in the business because of its close relationship with its audience.

You, too, have got to keep a keen eye on how you're doing. There's a bumper sticker you sometimes see on the backs of trucks: "How am I driving?" and an invitation to call an 800 number and make a report. "How am I doing?" is critical information. It can act as an early-warning system if you're veering off track. It can provide affirmation and bolster self-esteem. Take all audience feedback very seriously, from your bi-annual corporate review to the casual, "Hey, this looks terrific!" to no comment where comment is called for.

There are occasions when you can solicit feedback, but be careful not to sound needy or as if you're fishing for compliments or affirmation. Hand in your storyboard with a note that says, "I'm looking forward to your input," or even "What do you think?" When you make a presentation for your department at a meeting of department heads, take in not only your audience's comments but evidence of their emotional response. Did they seem enthusiastic, surprised, annoyed? Say your screenplay is turned down by the agent you hoped would represent it. She writes back, "Sorry, it doesn't really work for me." Call her immediately while the story is still in her mind and ask her if she can be a little more specific. She may refuse, but she just might tell you something important about why she doesn't want to buy your product.

Where Can You Find Your Audience?

Remember that what you are looking for is also looking for you. Think about where your audience is likely to be searching for you, and be there! Mary Beth will look for Web design firms on the Internet. She'll consult the *411 Directory* and the *Hollywood Creative Directory*'s new media edition, both invaluable resources for the entertainment industry. She'll call business school classmates and clients from previous jobs. She'll network for leads. She'll visit online headhunters like monster.com, hotjobs.com, or jobs.com. She'll be bold and call the heads of studios and television networks' Web design departments. And she'll ask for freelance work if there's no full-time employment available.

Jillian has created a list of every business in her community with which she feels some empathic draw or familiarity—the garden shop, the bookstore, the more expensive boutiques and gift shops, the town's one upscale clothing store, the jeweler's, the several art galleries, and the other restaurants in town—just because she's the expert in that field.

My secret for finding customers over the years has been trade shows. In my industry they represent a showcase for individual cable networks and technology companies—exactly the people I want to do business with. In addition to the enormous booths that show off each network's programming and promotional materials, there are panel discussions and seminars where I can schmooze with people who love television as much as I do. The cumulative effect is networking as an art form.

At Turner, I made it a point to meet my colleagues from other networks at these shows. I was truly interested in how they functioned in their jobs and was eager to share ideas. My interest was genuine, and my authenticity encouraged positive responses. I made a lot of friends at trade parties, at workshops, and on the convention floor. If I didn't know someone, I'd ask to be introduced. Sometimes I introduced myself.

When I decided to leave Turner Broadcasting to start my own agency, I took the opportunity at a cable convention to ask friends at other networks if they'd hire me if I were to go out on my own. I got a contract with Discovery Networks and Hanna-Barbera (a Turner-owned animation company) months before I took the leap. Those first two accounts provided me with a financial underpinning, and with courage. I couldn't have made the move without them.

In the months following my departure, I used the cable shows as a platform to build my brand and my business among old and new cable friends. Even today, almost ten years later, I tote my portfolio from booth to booth selling existing clients and finding new ones.

Sell them once, then never stop selling.

Once you know what you have to sell and have identified your target audience, finding where the audience hangs out requires a minimal amount of sleuthing. Almost every industry, from Agriculture to Zoology, has its equivalent of trade shows. Web sites like tsnn.com is an enormous trade show resource listing thousands of business events. *Go to trade shows.* They keep you plugged in and connected to your target audience. I tell every woman I meet: Attend every convention, forum, seminar, and workshop you can get your company to pay for. Then get up the courage to make an impression with as many people there as you can. (Steps Six and Seven in this book are all about making an impression.) It will help you in terms of getting new ideas, finding a new job, getting ahead in your industry, or building your own business.

Getting out is the only way to really get in.

Most industries have associated trade magazines. I know many women who subscribe to several trade publications and read them at home, and carry one with them in case they get stuck waiting somewhere, and keep at least one in the car for the same reason.

And most industries have a presence on the Internet. Cisco System's job page gets 500,000 hits a month. There are frequent seminars in your area of interest advertised in public forums like local newspapers and radio. Local colleges and universities offer classes that are career-specific, and there are job fairs and classes and coaches and counselors specializing in the job search, entrepreneurship, and career success. (Career counseling, by the way, is becoming a fast-growing specialty among therapists, who use their fundamental understanding of psychological types to help individuals find the most suitable jobs.)

You'll notice that when you focus on identifying your audience you'll begin to see references, leads, and cues everywhere. There are signs all around—all you have to do is tune in. From these resources you can refine your search to come up with the names of corporations and career-specific businesses and services. And from here you're a whole lot closer to finding out the name of the individual you need to talk to or write to about getting in the door.

There are a lot of careers where geography is a significant factor in locating the broadest possible customer base, but it's rarely necessary to relocate in order to do work you love to do and evolve a successful career. America's financial center is considered Wall Street in New York, but every city has banking or other financial institutions, and every major corporation has its own financial center. The movie industry is mostly in Los Angeles but in fact movies are made and movie production occurs in most states in this country, as well as internationally. Silicon Valley is the heart of the computer industry, but maybe not for much longer. The computer industry has a growing presence in Texas, Massachusetts, Colorado, and throughout the South and is emerging in every American city these days. If you really want to make it big, go where the action is. But Mary Beth, Jillian, and Laura could become powerful brands anywhere. And so can you.

Mastering the Law of Attraction

Depending on the product and on the customer, a company may advertise its brand in traditional vehicles such as print, on television and radio, or on-line on any variety of Web sites. Billboards attract customers' attention to brand products. The city museum that's trying to establish its brand promotes itself on the sides of buses.

On the other hand, more and more marketing dollars are going toward untraditional kinds of advertising at the grassroots level. In some of the rural towns that Clover-brand dairy products serves in the San Francisco Bay area, Clo, the well-known cartoon cow appreciated for her bad puns, hands out free ice cream at county fairs and on parade days. The customers line up for Clo.

Some companies will launch these untraditional or guerrilla promotional campaigns to get a buzz going, to get people talking about their product. Word of mouth is gold. You want nothing less. Pierre Mornell writes about someone who leafletted every car in the parking lot of Apple Computer's headquarters with a cover note and copy of his résumé.[2] (He got his interview, but not the job.) That's not my style, but the stunt communicated a lot about this guy's brand—slightly outrageous, someone who "thinks different," which is what Apple's tagline asks us to do.

Here's another unusual method that a friend of a friend used for self-promotion:

The Value of a Name Tag

Connie was already a successful actress and a recent MBA whose goal was to learn more about movie production. Through a contact in the industry, she got the opportunity to visit the set of *Mama Flora's Family* while the mini-series was being filmed in Atlanta. Her purpose was to observe the production process. Figuring it would be a good idea if people knew her name, she wore a self-stick name badge. As she went around the set asking questions and watching how things work, people were able to refer to her by name. A few days later Connie got a call from the head of production. A crew member hadn't shown up for work that day and the production manager thought of her. Even though she had never asked for a job, she was invited to work for them for the remainder of the shoot!

Rosalie Osias also put herself out there. She's a real estate lawyer, and targeting the banking industry as the customer she wanted she ran a yearlong series of provocative ads in various conservative banking magazines. In one ad she posed in a tuxedo and spike heels wielding a golf club. In another she was a cowboy with a cigar. Maybe the most outrageous had her reclining on a conference table in blouse and Ally McBeal short skirt with the caption, "Does this law firm have a reputation? You bet it does."[3]

Her campaign was gutsy and very controversial, and earned her national and international attention, not all of it complimentary. But Rosalie Osias got exactly the banking clients she wanted out of it, and the campaign helped build her brand to reflect the maverick she is.

Most of us won't leaflet a parking lot or buy billboard space. We're not going to give it away, like Clo the dairy cow, and we're probably not going to match Rosalie Osias for audacity. But we've definitely got to put ourselves in a direct line of sight of our target audience.

If you know your prospective client or employer is a workaholic, have lunch delivered to his or her desk with a note inside the bag asking for an appointment—maybe even include a "menu" of your capabilities.

My friend Barbara told me a story about a friend of a friend who was trying to get in the door at Young & Rubicam in New York in the sixties. The friend's brother raised homing pigeons as a hobby, and she borrowed one and had it delivered to the president of Y&R, along with a letter requesting an appointment. "Please specify date and time convenient for you," she wrote, "and insert this information in the canister on the bird's ankle. Then toss the bird out the window."

Less guerrilla-like tactics include "advertising" ourselves on a headhunter's Web site, on job search on-line bulletin boards, in trade magazines, and in the business section of newspapers. We advertise ourselves when we arrive at a trade show totally *on.* Our résumé and portfolio are pure advertisement. (Much more about this in Step Six, on packaging.) Volunteering to serve on a committee in your industry trade association is great for visibility. So is public speaking.

Mary Beth

Mary Beth figured the best way to advertise herself as a Web designer would be to design a knockout Web site of her own. She included footage of herself dressed in a black jersey and black capris, her long straight blond hair held back with a tortoiseshell barrette, guiding the viewer through a brightly colored wonderland of geometric hallways and various painted door-ways, behind which existed different aspects of herself: her work history, her education, her thoughts about where the Internet is going, her interest in art, her key attributes.

She also included her mission statement and her vision of what she would bring an employer or client. In the "Mail Room" you could contact her directly from the site by opening a window that would send E-mail, or by clicking on a "Let's Talk" icon to leave a voice message. The site was animated and colorful, and she played her role as tour guide with a kind of graceful confidence that surprised her.

Then Mary Beth E-mailed her targets to introduce herself and invite them to her site, which they could visit through a link in her E-mail. There were, it turned out, several Web design firms that specialized in launching new sites for the entertain-ment industry.

Every single one of them E-mailed her back to set up an ap-pointment.

Jillian

After compiling her list of those small and medium-sized busi-nesses in her community that she thought she'd like to work with, Jillian sent each of them a letter describing the services she would be offering, and inviting inquiries. Jillian's list in-cluded a dozen that she'd really love to do business with, and another six or seven that were also appealing. She only needed five to retain her services in order to achieve her goal. In most cases, she knew the proprietors personally, could call them by their first names, and was able to personalize her letters so each one was a little different from the others. Whether or not she got a response, she planned to follow up each letter with a phone call. Even if the majority of business owners had no need of her services, these calls were a way of connecting to the greater community, of getting the word out into the universe.

Laura

Laura decided to blitz her bosses with a brand campaign that would keep her name in front of them, and play up her value as a coach and communications specialist. The first thing she did was ask those executives who had used her over the last six months to write short, appreciative testimonials.

Then she put together a monthly one-page newsletter, focusing on the power of effective presentations, including an interesting article culled from newspapers or the Internet on the subject; high points of recent company presentations; and a "my most embarrassing moment" feature, solicited from company execs and management, which soon became the company favorite.

And she pitched the company's partners to provide a biannual workshop for management on developing presentation skills, and learning how to measure audience response.

You can also attract your audience by demonstrating the need you can fulfill, the problem you can solve, the benefit you can provide—even when the audience didn't know it had a need or a problem that needed solving. This is how I got my first "real" job, and how I've landed many accounts.

My First Job

Being president of my sorority at the University of Alabama had many advantages. One of them was that I got to meet the very successful parents of pledges. In February of my senior year, one such parent stood at our front door with his hands planted squarely on his daughter's shoulders. He presented her like a gift. "This is Ann," he said. "I'd like to see the president." We had lunch together, and I did my pitch on the university and sisterhood. Ann's father, Al Levenson, asked me what my future plans were. I told him about my dream of getting into the music business and a big grin lit up his face. "That's great," he said. "I own the largest chain of record stores in the South!" And he told me to come see him about a job when I was ready.

My dad taught me to seize opportunity when it presents itself, so a few days later I jumped in my car and went to visit Ann's father in Atlanta. He was very nice, but had to admit that he didn't have any specific job in mind, and was at a loss as to what I could do for him. I decided on the spot to create a job for myself.

I started asking him questions about his stores, Turtle's Records & Tapes. There were forty. What kind of advertising did he use? Who coordinated advertising among the stores? What kind of special events had they tried? I learned that he had no one to coordinate his advertising, manage special events, or create in-store signage. I jumped at the chance to do all that for a starting salary of $15,000, which seemed like a fortune to me, and was actually good money back then for an entry-level position. Best of all, I didn't have to start at the bottom as someone else's assistant, or as a sales clerk.

I stayed there almost three years and that job evolved into something incredibly exciting. When I left the company we had over one hundred stores in three states, an in-house newsletter that I wrote, and an in-house advertising agency that I built and managed. I was twenty-three years old and on my way.

Putting yourself in the target audience's line of sight sometimes means entering the fray. It means job interviews if your target audience is a corporation. It means time on the Internet to research a company before your interview. It means heavy networking—75 to 85 percent of all jobs are found as a direct result of networking. It means positioning yourself differently and decidedly better. Laura's plan to put her name in front of her bosses is a way to change her position in their eyes from a competent, hardworking employee to an important partner in their overall marketing effort. Though she's called an in-house consultant, she's looking to position herself as a corporate strategist. Jillian is changing her position from bookkeeper to business manager. And Mary Beth is making a radical change of position, from account executive to designer, and from one side of the country to another.

Some of this may seem like a trivial matter of semantics, but words are the defining tool for positioning a brand to attract its target audience.

Check Out the Competition

There's another aspect to the marketplace that every good brand must be attentive to. The market is where you meet your competition—those other products similar to your own. These are not just other job applicants and companies out to get your clients, they are your colleagues and co-workers as well.

Just as we need to know our audience thoroughly, we must also stay aware of what our "competition" is up to, whether we're engaged in a conscious contest or not. You can bet that Pepsi keeps its eyes on Coca-Cola.

This means staying plugged in. Keep up with the news in your industry. At those same trade shows where you're peddling your wares, keep your eyes open for other players.

Contrary to what you might think, competition is not necessarily a bad thing. Brands need competition in order to distinguish themselves by being better than or offering something more than or different from their competition. Also, today's competition may be tomorrow's partnership, as merger madness continues into the twenty-first century.

Al and Laura Ries remind us of "The Law of Fellowship" in *The*

22 Immutable Laws of Branding: "In order to build the category, a brand should welcome other brands." "Choice stimulates demand," say the Rieses. "Customers respond to competition because choice is seen as a major benefit. If there is no choice, customers are suspicious. Maybe the category has some flaws? Maybe the price is too high? Who wants to buy a brand if you don't have another brand to compare it with?"[4]

This is why you find a "garment district" or an "auto row" or the café scene each in its own neighborhood—to encourage customers to shop around. What's also nice about these neighborhoods is that the separate shops and emporiums within them are as open to one another as to their customers, and it becomes fairly easy to know what the others in their category are doing.

We need to look for similar neighborhoods in our category. The trade show is one. The Internet is definitely another. I keep track of what other agencies are producing for the digital world by reading my trade magazines, the *L.A. Times,* the *Wall Street Journal,* and *Business Week.*

Mary Beth

Aside from keeping up with industry news in papers, trade shows, and on-line, Mary Beth will keep track of her classmates from Kellogg and Parsons, many of whom were dedicated to becoming players in the digital world. Those out in the job market will represent her competition.

Jillian

Jillian got familiar with her competition when she chatted by phone with the bookkeeping and financial services in her market, and she scans the "fictitious business names" applications in the local weekly for new businesses, which are more often potential new clients than potential new competition.

Laura

Because there's only one presentation specialist at Laura's company and she's it, she has no competition at work, but still she needs to stay aware of what other presentation specialists are doing. There are several companies that perform the same function Laura does in-house. If she weren't getting results, any of her executives could hire outside help with their presentations.

Competition may be just the thing to make things interesting for your audience and keep you on your toes, but you'd be in deep denial if you didn't admit that competition may also create a major barrier to success. In the next chapter, we'll look at the major brand barriers you're liable to encounter on the career track, competition among them, and learn some graceful sidesteps and some winning moves to divert them.

Step 3 Exercises:
All About Your Revered Target Audience

1. WHO IS MY TARGET AUDIENCE?

The "target audience" is your customer, the entity who pays your salary. Your target will exist within an industry, like one of those listed below, and many others that you can think of:

Accounting	Health Care	Travel/Tourism
Apparel	Employment	Education
Illustration	Construction	Agricultural
Finance	Paper Products	Graphic arts
Computers	Real Estate	Interior design
Party Planning	Transportation	Engineering
Manufacturing	Fashion	Food & beverage
Oil Products	Aerospace	Catering
Publishing	Fine arts	Law
Retail	Aviation	Jewelry
Civil Service	Science	Pharmaceuticals
Technology	Medicine	Research
Advertising	Hospitality	Entertainment
Architecture	Insurance	Social service
Automotive	Metalwork	Internet
Broadcasting	PR/Marketing	Music
Nutrition	Recreation	

Identify your industry, and then begin to narrow your focus. What kind of manufacturing? Is your target audience a wholesaler or a retailer? Is it the creative or analytical end of the industry? Can you narrow it even further? Ideally, focus

(CONTINUES)

on a particular company and department, or a particular clientele or audience, and record your brand's target audience here:

_____

_____

_____

2. What Do I Want My Audience to Think of Me?

Write a statement from the point of view of your prospective client, customer, or employer that focuses on precisely what you want your target audience to think when they hear your name:

_____

_____

_____

Keeping track of the target audience means monitoring how your brand is doing in the marketplace. Be prepared with ways to solicit such feedback without sounding like you're fishing for compliments. Jot them down here:

_____

_____

_____

3. Where Is My Audience?

Search the Web. Read the trades. Make a list of trade shows in your field. Attend every convention, forum, seminar, and workshop you can. List ways that you will network like crazy:

_____

_____

_____

4. ATTRACTING MY AUDIENCE

Ask yourself, How can I increase my visibility? Decide on a plan for advertising yourself to your target audience. Make a To Do list that you can check off as you accomplish each item. For example:

- Post résumé
    a. on a headhunter's Web site,
    b. on job search on-line bulletin boards,
    c. in trade magazines,
    d. in the business section of newspapers.

- Volunteer at industry-sponsored event.

- Other:

Whenever possible, create your own job based on meeting a need or solving a problem that you observe. There's almost always a need or a problem.

5. COMPETITION IN THE MARKETPLACE

Your target audience has many suitors, but this is not bad. They're out there, visible, not an unknown quantity. You have the opportunity to size up your competition, which you should most certainly do, and to distinguish yourself from them, which you must also do. Do your research. Find out about as many direct competitors as you can, then list them with a brief description of their strengths and weaknesses.

_____

_____

_____

(CONTINUES)

Now list your brand's attributes that set you apart from the competition:

_____

_____

_____

4

Don't Crash and Burn— Figure Out What's Stopping You

With a new awareness and appreciation of your talents, a powerful mission, and a clear understanding of your target audience, your brand's on the launch pad with both engines firing. So, what's stopping you? Could it be the uncharted territory ahead, or those meteors you can just barely see off in the distance?

Well, you're right—there are obstacles out there, big and small, and of more than one variety. In creating a brand strategy for a product, a careful analysis is undertaken to determine principal barriers—those market conditions that can keep a product from achieving success, like the brand's competition, timing, financing, location, and lack of consumer demand, to name a few.

Although similar external circumstances can definitely have a negative effect on a personal brand, the fact that we're human and female means there's a whole other range of psychological issues that can rub some of the edge off the brand we're building.

At this point in creating a powerful brand, your next challenge is to *identify what's stopping you.* Take a good look at the two lists that follow. Does anything look familiar?

External Barriers	*Internal Barriers*
gender biases	fear of the unknown
financial circumstances	shyness/easily embarrassed
competition	moodiness/depression, anger
timing	self-limiting ideas
location	lack of confidence/fear of failing
lack of demand	family myths
bad luck	fear of success
family expectations	being too comfortable/fear of change
lack of experience	perfectionism/fear of chaos
saboteurs	balancing work and family/fear of failing one or the other

When Fear Rears Its Ugly Head

As you can see from the list of internal obstacles, fear rears its ugly head in a variety of ways. I don't care what it is, if you're scared to do something then you're going to take every opportunity to avoid doing it now or anytime in the near future. Fear stops you in your tracks. It's critical to overcome these inner fears while developing your brand strategy because in many cases the thing you're afraid to do is in fact the one thing you *need* to do to solidify your brand. Isn't it funny how that works?

When I left Turner Broadcasting to start my own agency, my biggest fear was of failing. I was giving up the security I always craved, my nice office, two trips a month to New York, a stock purchase plan, my 401K, health benefits, and let's not forget the regular paycheck—for a totally uncertain future. If I failed I'd have to go back to the corporate world, which I passionately wanted out of. If I failed, it would put me in a very precarious financial situation. If I failed, I thought I'd be humiliated. For sure I'd be a major disappointment to myself.

When I look at the list of internal barriers, I see that my fears had to do with the unknown, with a lack of confidence in myself and in the universe, and with being awfully comfortable, and a little scared of change. If my fears had been bigger than my determination I might never have left Turner at all.

Create a No-Fear Zone

Your brand goes nowhere when fear rules. You've got to get on top of your fears, or through them, or past them and into a place called the No-Fear Zone. This is a great place to be—you and your brand will flourish here—but it's not easy to get into, and it's definitely not easy to stay in once you're there. Circumstances are constantly throwing things at you, knocking you out of this safe place, and every time you're bumped out, you've got to scramble and rebuild in order to get back in.

Although there isn't a password, there are some things you can do to facilitate your entry and staying power in a No-Fear Zone.

OBSESS OVER YOUR GOAL, whether it's to start your own business, or get ahead in your company, or to change careers, or to attract new business or better projects, or simply to build your brand's image and reputation. The more you think about what you're doing, the more familiar it all becomes. The more familiar, the less fearful. Talk about your goal with your friends and family. Dream about it. Visualize it. Write about it. Work on it.

ANTICIPATE CHALLENGES AND OVERPREPARE FOR THEM. For months before I left Turner, I began socking away money. I sat down and calculated how much I needed to make, and took a serious look at my expenses. I knew I'd have to put money into a home office, and I figured out what it was going to cost. By the time I did leave my corporate job, I thought there'd be few start-up costs I hadn't anticipated, and therefore few surprises to knock me out of my No-Fear Zone—and I was right.

ASK YOURSELF "WHAT'S THE WORST THAT CAN HAPPEN?" What's the worst that can happen if your worst fears come true? Could you live with it? How bad could it really be? For me, total failure would have meant going back to a corporate job. Big deal.

I recently took a "Quantum Leap" workshop with Tessa Warschaw, Ph.D., to learn a little more about facing what frightens us. She's created a terrific tool for diffusing fear, which she calls a "Disaster Fantasy" sheet. At the end of this chapter we'll take some time to play out a disaster fantasy on paper. Notice what happens to fear when it confronts "the worst that can happen."

IN SPITE OF FEAR, PRACTICE THE POWER OF BEING POSITIVE. Fear is a big fat negative force that loses power when confronted by positive circumstances, whether it's a positive mind-set on your part, or a positive impression someone else has of you. A branded product is always trying to demonstrate its most positive qualities or key benefits to create a positive impression. It practices the power of the positive in its advertising, in its packaging or presentation, in its associations. The most successful brands are those that score the highest positives when it comes to what their target audiences think of them and "feel" about them. A brand's upbeat tagline is designed to trigger a positive emotional response from its customers. Even when you're fearful, think positively.

FACE OFF WITH WHAT YOU FEAR. So finally I was ready. I took a deep breath and gave my notice at Turner, and three months later walked away from my nice safe job. And you know what? Turner became my first client, eventually paying me yearly consulting fees larger than my entire salary as a full-time employee. Go figure.

The Confidence Game

SELF-CONFIDENCE, AND THE APPEARANCE OF SELF-CONFIDENCE, IS A BRAND'S MOST POWERFUL BARRIER-BUSTER. The confident mind-set is an incredible propeller in all aspects of life; it allows us to move forward into unexplored territories even in spite of our fears and enables us to take risks—and for these reasons it's especially important in the business world.

Check out some of the world's most powerful brands. BMW, Nike, IBM, Disney, Coke: Every one of them is telling us, "You can't do better than me! In my category, I'm the best there is!" And because these brands back up their expressions of confidence in themselves with great products, with great value, with fabulous service, their customers believe them. Confidence is a self-fulfilling prophecy.

Confidence is also wildly attractive. Customers flock to the confident brand. And this is also the case for most of the successful businesswomen I know, who seem to have tons of confidence—and most of the time they do. But you'd have to be a stone not to lose confidence now and then, especially in the workplace where competition is high. Loss of confidence can bring down the walls of your No-Fear Zone in about three seconds, so maintaining confidence in yourself, and maintaining other people's confidence in your brand, is critical to any success.

The Comedian

Several years ago, an unknown comedian came to Los Angeles to make it in entertainment. No matter what he did, or how many comedy clubs he performed at, he couldn't get a break—or even very many laughs. Still, this comedian held on to his confidence. He knew he was funny. Really, really funny. If he ever felt as if he wasn't going to make it, he'd shove the thought aside and take his car (which was also his residence) up to the top of the Hollywood Hills. There he'd look down at the town where he wanted to be a star, and at the very top of his lungs he'd shout, "YOU LOVE ME!"

That struggling comedian was Jim Carrey.

Shouting your value to the rooftops may work for you, too. Or you might want to try my system for keeping confidence intact and boosting it when you need to: *Keep a victory file with confidence-building reference points for yourself.* Save any excellent reviews, certificates of merit, letters of recommendation or appreciation or congratulations, and keep them in a "victory file." Make a note of verbal recognition, too, projects well-received, the admiration of your friends. And take the time to flip through it *regularly,* not just when your confidence wavers.

Mary Beth

Mary Beth posts her victory file on her Web site, in a virtual file cabinet in the room behind the door marked "Office," where visitors have the option of flipping through it, too. It contains a letter from her college dean recommending her to Parsons School of Design, a copy of her graduate degree, a thank-you note from a key client, and a video clip of her skydiving in Colorado.

Laura

Laura now saves a file on her computer desktop with all the positive E-mail she gets from within her company and from the outside vendors she works with, and she keeps a scrapbook for past issues of Laura's Letter, her new in-house newsletter.

Mariette Edwards, business and personal coach, and a treasured friend, described her "brag book," a variation on the victory file:

When I left the corporate world in 1989 I was confident and sure I could make a success out of my next endeavor. When my confidence started to slip, I borrowed an idea from an acquaintance and began to keep a record of every positive comment anyone made about me. I went a step further by creating my brag book, a three-ring binder that I filled with testimonial letters, handwritten notes, articles, and samples of my creative work. It started out as a half-inch binder that grew to one inch, then two inches, and now it's three inches and still growing. It's an immediate reminder of all the good I do. It's also very useful when meeting with a potential client.

Remember to review all such material before you apply for a raise, before an interview, before an important presentation, when you're worried about whether you're charging too much—any time your faith in your brand is the least bit shaky.

Dealing with Men

Most of the women I know who are working at the top are gender-blind. They don't consider themselves victims of a male-based system, they think of themselves as winners—and they are. Not only do I not hear women talking about men keeping them down, I see them engaging in working relationships that are clearly based on mutual admiration for what each can bring to the table. My perception is that what's going on between men and women at the top levels in business is about getting the job done, and not about gender bias.

But there's no denying the disparity between men and women in the workplace, and here it is: *Men are promoted based on potential. Women are promoted based on performance.* As I see it, that is *the* big gender issue at work. It may not be fair, it may not be conscious, but that's the way it is, at least until American corporations become convinced of the unique benefits women have to offer. And this is guaranteed to happen. It's already beginning to happen. But until the conversion is complete, these are the rules of the game.

Once we get it—that performance is the answer—we can get on with our lives and begin moving up the ladder in our careers. In fact, there's an opportunity here to actually demonstrate the strength of our brand and its best qualities in every project we take on. Marketing guru Tom Peters (author of *In Search of Excellence*) says that "all white-collar work is project work" and it's projects that can make you a star. Projects are the vehicles from which you can demonstrate consistency, creativity, reliability, and productivity—all essential components of any successful personal brand. Projects are the opportunity to perform like crazy and really up your stock by showing what passion, talent, and commitment you bring to the job.

Women thrive when we are operating in our strengths.

While men are about winning, women are about collaborating, creating win-win relationships. We have natural talents like patience, intuition, multi-tasking, networking, and nurturing—powerful leadership qualities for making any business grow. Trust in these inbred qualities. Use them in your working life. Don't ever try to hide them or disguise them.

Nina DiSesa, chairman and chief creative officer of McCann-Erickson, the world's largest ad agency, admits she's very comfortable with her masculine qualities—she enjoys both competition and confrontation. But she plays both down, finding her "feminine traits—empathy and collaboration" of more value in her job.

In an interview in *Fortune* magazine, she says, "I'm dealing with big egos, big personalities. Fragile, high-maintenance people. If I didn't have a strong nurturing component, I couldn't do it."[1]

The Backlash of Being Little Miss Perfect

Working to do things right is one thing; striving for perfection is another. Perfectionism is one response to the fear of chaos. By doing things perfectly we're attempting to maintain order. Although there can be value in it, perfectionism is a principal barrier because it's more often another place where women get stuck. Symptoms of perfectionism are rewriting and rewriting and rewriting a report, often becoming less confident with every new version. Or rethinking, or neatening, or categorizing, or reorganizing—all these are subtle tactics that can keep you moving in place instead of moving ahead. When you find yourself working harder in these ways, you're probably not working smarter and you can bet that your brand will suffer.

Successful people with strong brands keep their eyes on the big picture and don't get seduced by the details. Perfectionism can bog you down in details, and in this way can overwhelm objectivity, which can be disastrous in business.

Jillian

Jillian is one of those people who want everything they do to be perfect, according to their exceedingly high specifications for perfection. When things don't go exactly as she's envisioned them, she's disappointed in herself. This is true in her cooking, her gardening, her music, and her work. But how many things ever go just as we picture them? Jillian's perfectionism has kept her down—and I mean that in two ways: What she counts as her lack of perfection depresses her, and her depression keeps her from moving ahead.

The kind of depression I'm talking about is not necessarily emotional. It can be more like a rut, which is why it took Jillian years to take control of her financial destiny in spite of all that she knows about practical financial matters.

Laura

Laura is also a perfectionist. She's rarely home before 8:00 P.M. during the work week. Weekends are her only time to really connect with her children, but instead of playing on Saturday or going on a family outing, if she hasn't brought work home from the office she'll do a top-to-bottom cleaning job on her house. She could hire someone to come in once a week to free herself up for family fun, but she says there's no one who can clean as thoroughly as she can.

Even if it were achievable, perfectionism would still be an unnecessary extravagance. The whole trick to softening or finding balance for a perfectionistic nature is to not get stuck in surface stuff. Put your do-it-right energy into the things that really count and do the rest "well enough."

The Balancing Act: Work and Family

There are a million of these stories: the husband who thinks his wife should be home raising children and doesn't want her to work; the in-laws who have a similar idea of the role of wife and mother; the husband who likes the security of his wife's corporate job and discourages her from making any changes that might rock the boat; the kids who feel deprived because Mom is never home; the mom who feels deprived for the same reason; the spouse who feels like second fiddle to the other's job; the one who's jealous of the other's relationships at work.

If you're an ambitious person with a passion to succeed, and the ones you love aren't with you all the way, it can break your heart. It can undermine your confidence with guilt. Sometimes the conflicts between work and family can tear the family apart. All this makes success very difficult.

But if you're someone who seeks success and your family supports you, and applauds you, and loves you, and makes you laugh when you've had a miserable day, and offers you a massage, or dinner out, it can restore you and bind you closer than ever, and it can directly affect your ability to succeed.

Any of us who work absolutely have to think about our priorities where family is concerned. Make a declaration of how you and your partner see yours, like Laura and her husband have done:

A Declaration of Commitment and Intent

Joe and I are committed to one another, and to our separate careers.

We've agreed to keep each other current on what's happening in our work, so that we can share the ups and downs together.

We agree to honor our commitment to our work, but will always try not to let work get in the way of our commitment to ourselves and our family.

We've agreed to invest 10 percent of each of our salaries in our children's college funds.

We've agreed to arrange vacation schedules so we can take them as a family.

Things change. People change. Jobs change. Feelings change. But Laura and Joe have declared their best intentions and their shared dream that actually has form in a written agreement, and from that point of solidarity it's easier to work out differences that come up later. Addressing their intentions, they've established a line of communication on the subject of family and work that can serve as a lifeline down the road.

Make Your Family Part of Your Team

I used to sit at the dining-room table with my dad and help him while he laid out ads. Think of a way you can let your kids engage and participate in your work life beyond the occasional visit to the office. For instance, when my friend Barbara has to put together a press kit, she lays out all the material and lets her six-year-old son do the collating. She takes her eight-year-old daughter shopping with her for presentation folders and has never yet had to overrule her decisions. Over supper, she talks to her husband and kids about her day. She shares her thoughts about a report due the next week. After supper she may try on a couple of outfits. Should she wear the blue or gray suit to the board meeting tomorrow, and which shoes? She celebrates her achievements with her family. All of them are proud of her.

Laura

Laura recruits her ten- and twelve-year-old to watch the corporate video presentations she creates for her bosses. If she can hold her kids' attention for a twenty-minute infomercial, she knows she's got something that's going to be a winner.

I know a single mom who's a motivational speaker and her kids are her most invaluable audience and focus group. She rehearses new material with them, and they review her taped presentations and then fill out a questionnaire about how she looked, how she sounded, her content. If there was an audience, there are questions about what the kids got from the audience response. She gets great brand advice and information from them, and they feel very plugged into her life and what's important to her.

My friend Sukie is a therapist who specializes in the area of death and dying. Her father was an oncologist who had long, serious "consultations" with Sukie when she was six, seven, and eight years old. He'd review his more difficult cases with her, explain his thinking to her, ask her advice. He didn't talk baby talk. He spoke clinically, but with explanations. No doubt these think-aloud sessions helped the doctor decide for himself the best course of treatment for a patient, but they were almost indescribably precious times for a little girl who adored her father and has known his respect for her opinions all her life.

I don't try to balance work and family. I never have. In my life they're all mixed up. I don't shut it off when I close the door to my office and walk around the corner to my house. I bring it inside and let it pull up a chair. My husband and I talk about it over dinner. It would seem weird to me to drop it at the door, and my family would feel left out if I didn't share this incredibly important aspect of my life with them.

Of course we have to promise to be responsible and act responsibly. But women generally take their responsibilities seriously. Not many of us are likely to run off and leave our kids while we go on a two-month archeological dig in Turkey, if that was our work. But we might figure out a way to bring them along for the adventure of a lifetime.

Except in extreme cases, I don't believe we have to sacrifice our family for our career or our career for our family. Our husbands don't.

But we do have to realize that we won't be perfect at all three jobs—being wife and mother and businesswoman. Superwoman is not only dead, she never lived. Today we're just trying to manage the chaos, not control it or make it go away.

We'd be kidding if we said this particular juggling act was easy. But God made women with the ability to multi-task. We are amazing at keeping ten balls in the air. It's when we get caught in the details and try to be perfect that we may drop a ball. And we're not so good about giving ourselves a break when that happens.

If you've got to juggle, my advice is to trim down from ten balls in the air to eight or six. Cut your social obligations in half. Don't feel as if you have to cross everything off today's list before you leave the office. Prioritize that list: What has to be done and what can wait? Your husband and children can't wait. While you don't live for them alone, they need you home at a decent hour, interested in them, with love in your heart and energy in reserve.

When Your Brand Is Brand-New

This potential roadblock from the External Barriers list is one we all have to live through. Mary Beth had never been a Web designer before, although she had the skills. She'd never worked in the computer industry. She'd never lived in California. Even branded products start out new and customers have to take a chance on them. The new brand compensates by trying to distinguish itself from the tired old brands everyone's used to by making itself bigger, or sportier, or more expensive, or less expensive than the already established competition.

You can distinguish yourself by marketing your brand's lack of experience as an advantage. Mary Beth will play up her fresh outlook. She's brand new, and newness is an attraction. Hiring managers are aware that new people may be more eager to prove themselves than the more experienced players and often prove the hardest workers. Everybody's looking to discover new talent. Why shouldn't it be you?

Also, experience is nice, but it's not everything. Mary Beth may lack experience but have something much better to offer, and this might be her natural talent, or her point of view, or her attitude, or her dedication. The fact that she's focused on the entertainment industry can also make up for her lack of experience. There may be plenty of Web designers to talk to, but if only one or two of them identify themselves as dedicated to your particular industry, wouldn't you call them first?

The first time I took on a project to brand a cable network, I had no previous experience, but cable networks were so new that hardly anybody else had any experience either. That niche was just cracking open, just as the Internet is today, and offering a gold mine of opportunity for both entrepreneurs and those inside the corporate culture.

Be a Good Girl Scout: Prepare for the Unexpected

You're on your way to the interview and there's an accident on the freeway and you're delayed two hours. Or you're just on your way out the door to the meeting and day care calls to say that little Lucinda has a fever. Or you sent your bid in by messenger, and the messenger decided to quit for the day before he delivered it. These are those things you couldn't have anticipated—the natural disasters that always happen at the most inopportune times.

Things happen. Mostly they're very haphazard. But you can, at least to some degree, protect against many things that look like they're beyond your control but aren't really. You can carry a cell phone, for instance, in case there's the accident on the freeway, so you can at least call the interviewer and let her know the situation. You can have a backup system in place for children's crises—your husband, a nanny, a friend, a neighbor. You can use a bonded, responsible messenger service.

Crisis management is a key component to a company's brand strategy. Overcoming uncontrollable circumstances has become an artform. To protect their brands against the fallout from unexpected crises, many companies have a damage control task team that flies into action to appease the customer. In the summer of 1999, Coca-Cola was a little too slow in deploying damage control when people in Europe began getting sick after drinking Coke. The crisis wasn't treated as a high priority for many days, there was no apology from Coke executives for more than a week after the news broke, and when the company finally did begin to respond, it seemed to try to downplay the reports of illness. Big mistake.

Coke's stock lost 25 percent of its value in the months following the disaster, and its money losses were estimated in the tens of millions of dollars in Europe. But the damage to customer loyalty, more valuable than money or stock, is inestimable. Coke would have done a whole lot better by saying, "Whoa, we've got a problem!" and taking action right away. Take a lesson from it. When a crisis arises and you're caught in circumstances beyond your control, say so immediately. Honest and forthright communication is often the appropriate first response to brand crises.

Don't Forget to Look Over Your Shoulder

It may be true that competition is good for business, but it can also be devastating for business. When Amazon.com rolled onto the Internet, it rolled right over a lot of independent bookstores on the street. When Starbucks moves into the neighborhood, it's usually curtains for the corner coffee shop. A new cable network may threaten the established networks; a new sit-com on Fox is competition to the programs in the same time slot on ABC, NBC, and CBS.

Brand competition is great for the customer, providing a lot of choice and causing the competing brands to produce better and better products in their efforts to win the big prize, which is the love and loyalty of the customer.

This is exactly what happens to people like us, who are entering or already operating within the world of business. I'm out there, a brand strategist for the digital age, and there are other brand strategists out there, too. I've narrowed my competition by specializing in cable TV and the Internet, but there are still other agencies serving clients that fall inside my area of expertise. With rare exceptions, we've all got competition. You may not *feel* as if you're in competition with the fellow in the cubicle next to yours, but believe it. This should be one of the things that keeps us on our toes and motivates us to continue building our brands.

But toes get stepped on in business all the time, and competition can hurt because in any contest there's a winner and a loser. Almost all of us—and even the best of us—are going to lose some of the time. You can pretty much count on it.

I say if you've done your best, you can—and should—be proud of yourself even though the job or the account went to someone else. You're not a lesser human being for not winning the race, you're just not the fastest—today.

And in most losses there's a lesson, though it may be hard to spot right away. If you can learn why the job went to the other guy, it can only help your efforts the next time around. You may find out you were asking too much, or the client didn't think you had enough experience, or the other candidate's portfolio struck the hiring committee as more impressive. These are all potentially remediable.

You don't have to be a "competitive personality" to become a *great* competitor. Instead, use these very simple strategies in various combinations to *win:*

Beating the Competition

1. BE TRUE TO YOUR BRAND. Let your values shine through and you'll never go wrong.

2. GET TO WORK EARLY. You can get a huge amount of work done in the hour or so before normal business hours begin. In a corporate setting, the early bird is *always* noticed.

3. HAVE A GOOD ATTITUDE. My friend Cindy House at E! Entertainment Television attributes a good portion of her success with people in business to "my smile and my great attitude."

4. DON'T SUCK UP. Great brands don't agree for security's sake or to keep the peace. It's boring!

5. KEEP ON TOP OF WHAT'S HAPPENING IN YOUR WORLD. Read everything that's relevant to your business. Then when you're with colleagues, refer to something that you've read. It's won-

derful to be able to say, "Have you been following. . . ." Solid brands are always in the know.

6. GET IT DONE FASTER THAN ANYONE ELSE. We are way beyond the Age of Aquarius. This is the Digital Age and speed counts.

7. BE MORE COMMUNICATIVE THAN ANYONE ELSE. Have you ever ordered a book from Amazon.com? You get a confirmation E-mail within minutes, and then another notice, often the next day, saying the book has been shipped. If you ever have a question for them, they respond to all E-mail immediately. Be like them. Build brand loyalty through followup.

8. OVERDELIVER ON YOUR PROMISES. Do more than what you said you'd do.

9. PLAY FAIR. When you throw dirt you lose ground.

10. SURROUND YOURSELF WITH PEOPLE WHO SING YOUR PRAISES. Every brand wants to start a buzz. Great recommendations win the race.

When Someone's Out to Mess with Your Brand

There's another kind of barrier you can sometimes run into on the road to success that may be less obvious and possibly more insidious than any of the other obstacles we've looked at so far. That barrier is the *people* who would like us to think they have our best interests at heart but who may be subtly undermining our success. The saboteur has the advantage insofar as he is by definition, sneaky, so you may never even know he's out there spreading flat-out lies, or much more subtle gossip. Monica Lewinsky's nemesis, Linda Tripp, would be considered a brand leader in this category.

Sabotage is often inspired by jealousy, a subject most women know at least something about. In love, jealousy can break your heart. In the workplace it can kill you.

When I got pregnant last year, one of my competitors told *all my clients* that I'd probably be quitting after I had the baby.

I could hardly believe it when this news got back to me. So, seven months pregnant, I went to the biggest cable trade show of the year in Chicago to ask each of my clients for new projects, explaining the support system I'd arranged for myself to maintain and service their business. I picked up six new projects on the spot, I never mentioned my competitor's name, and he got branded "out of the loop."

A saboteur will draw attention to you, and though he may have intended it to be negative attention, you have the power to turn it to your advantage. At that trade show, people were curious, congratulatory, and interested in what I had to say. It was like having a captive audience, and it was the saboteur who had arranged it all and who had energized my appearance there with the incentive to protect my brand, my company, my future, myself.

Sabotage is an intentional attack on your reputation. This is what sabotage sounds like: "I agree, she's really talented, especially considering how much she drinks." Or "I don't know if there's any truth to it, but I've heard he has a substance abuse problem." "I really don't know why they keep him around. The old dog has really lost his edge." Or even, "Frankly, I think she's an impostor. Sooner or later she'll be found out." And in some circles, "Do you think he's gay?" is enough to change how people look at you.

Sabotage always comes with an ulterior motive, like eliminating a perceived threat, or building oneself up at someone else's expense. That's what Kendall-Jackson vintners, makers of fine wine, accused Gallo Winery of in 1997.

The Turning Leaf Story

What do you think of when you think of Gallo? Most people would answer "inexpensive," "jug wine," or "table wine."

The Gallo brand is so well-established as a lower-end beverage that in 1995, when the company wanted to market a slightly more expensive product, they decided not to put the Gallo name anywhere on the bottle. Instead, they branded their wine "Turning Leaf," and their label uses a large grape leaf in autumn colors on a white background. The leaf looks as if it's turning on a draft of air as it falls to earth. It's a very nice design.

When Gallo brought their wine to market, they paid their retail outlets for space on the shelves next to Kendall-Jackson wines.

Kendall-Jackson has used the same label for its Vintner's Reserve–brand wines for years. When you look for it on the shelf, you look for its large autumn-colored grape leaf. It isn't a falling leaf; it appears to lie flat on the white label and the Kendall-Jackson coat of arms covers a part of it, but it's used for all the Vintner's Reserve varieties, and it's been that brand's distinguishing mark that set it apart from all the other brands around it—until now.

Kendall-Jackson was outraged, and thought it was no coincidence that Gallo wanted to set up right next to them on the store shelf, and no accident that Gallo didn't want their name on their own label, and no accident that they were using the same flanged bottle that Kendall-Jackson used. The Kendall-Jackson attorneys accused Gallo of sabotage, of trying to create confusion over the two brands. Maybe Gallo didn't intend to damage Kendall-Jackson directly—although their brand certainly declined precipitously after Turning Leaf's appearance—but surely Gallo intended to benefit at Kendall-Jackson's expense.

Kendall-Jackson got a lot of positive publicity during the lawsuit they brought against Gallo, because the public perceived Gallo as the bad guy, which was nice for Kendall-Jackson—but Gallo prevailed in the courtroom. Today you can see both brands on grocers' shelves, often side by side.

There's also the kick-'em-while-they're-down kind of sabotage that a competitor may use when you're at a disadvantage, after a lost account or a conflict with an associate. Although I don't consider my pregnancy to have been a "disadvantage," my competitor tried to play on that perception by spreading gossip that could have hurt my business. I have a close friend who returned to her job as an assistant in a large architectural office after maternity leave to find everyone's attitude toward her changed. She had been with the company for two years, and had a warm relationship with everyone, as far as she knew. But all their warmth had been replaced by a deep chill. She never found out what the problem was, though she asked her boss directly. Ultimately, it was so unpleasant for her that she quit.

I can guarantee she had been zapped by a saboteur. The same kind of tactic happens between brand competitors all the time. After the Coke recall in Belgium in the summer of 1999, and while Coke was still struggling with damage control and suffering big financial losses as a result, its offices in four countries were raided by the European Commission. The commission was there to investigate complaints by Pepsico, Pepsi's parent company, along with other Coca-Cola competitors, that Coke was abusing its dominant position in the European market by using various illegal incentives to exclude them.

When You Throw Dirt You Lose Ground

It's not only your direct competitors who resort to sabotage. There are other people who are so insecure that they may engage in deception and innuendo. Usually, the karma police will eventually bust the saboteur, but that's not much consolation when you're the target.

The best defense against sabotage is to use your brand as a life raft. If you hold tight to your key attributes you *will* sail beyond the saboteur's influence.

Laura

Laura had withstood a saboteur in her career—the woman she replaced at her current job. I'll call her Samantha. Samantha had moved on to an even higher position at a much bigger packaged-goods company.

It wasn't long before Laura began to show her bosses how good she was, took on more projects, and added staff. Every industry being its own small world, Samantha soon heard about Laura's successes and began to get jealous. Laura certainly posed no threat to her, but Samantha didn't like the praise she was getting, and began speaking badly of Laura in the industry. "Well, I *saw* her résumé, and I know she wasn't completely honest . . ." She even tried to denigrate what Laura showed interest in. When she heard that Laura had gone to a particular workshop, she'd say something like, "I went there last year and got nothing out of it," as if whatever Laura was doing was a waste of time.

Although Laura knew what was going on, she wouldn't play. She kept a positive attitude, stayed enthusiastic in her job, did her best work. She never talked badly about the one who was talking badly about her, even though it was awful for her to walk into a conference room where she knew that at least some of the people had heard lies about her.

Samantha was in a position to do Laura great harm, but Laura's emerging brand served as her life raft. She held tight to her key attributes, her creative talent, her energy, her enthusiasm, and her high ethical standards, and ultimately sailed beyond where Samantha could hurt her. It's Samantha whose own brand was damaged—and badly—because it was so obvious that she couldn't stand someone outperforming her. She's still the talented individual she had been, but she's also been branded insecure, not very nice, and potentially dangerous. You can see people watching their back when they're around her now, and being more careful. Samantha will have to do some serious repair work on her brand to save it.

The moral to this story? The road to success is the high road. Be true to your brand—to yourself and your ideals. Don't engage in dirty stuff. The karma police will bust you.

Recognizing Symptoms of Sabotage

Not that I want you to be paranoid, but below are some signs that could signal danger. Use your natural intuition and intelligence to judge for yourself on a case-by-case basis.

- PERSONAL LIFE PERPETRATORS: Colleagues at work who are a little too interested in your life away from the office. I mean there's a certain amount of information we share, but sharing intimacies with other than intimate friends is a bad idea, especially at work.

- INSISTENT INSTIGATORS: People at work who try to get you to say something bad about someone, or try to get you to agree with their negative view of a third person. It could be a set-up.

- HOSTILE HUMILIATORS: Colleagues who seem hostile to your success, who don't congratulate you on your accomplishments. This is a flashing yellow light. Your real friends will be happy for your successes at every level, and should say so.

- FAKE FLAKES: People at work acting unnaturally toward you or avoiding you.

Personal boundaries are an absolute necessity for keeping yourself and your brand distinguished from the pack.

Don't get sucked in when you see the symptoms of sabotage. Learn how to protect yourself. Eliminate those "friends" or colleagues from your sphere who denigrate your success, or seem at all threatened by it.

This isn't the easiest thing when you're in the same office or at adjoining desks, but if you've gotten this far you've probably learned a few nonbrutal ways of discouraging unwanted intimacy. Use them *now*.

Try "Sorry, I can't talk," "Don't have time for lunch today," "I don't think I want to work on that one with you. I've got an idea I'm going to try on my own . . . ," or "I'm not ready to discuss it; I need to give it some more thought . . . ," and these "friends" will get the message and back off. Personal boundaries are necessary for preserving energy and keeping yourself and your brand set off from everyone else. Protect those boundaries.

Step 4 Exercises
Defend Against Brand Barriers

1. CONTINGENCY PLANNING FOR BRAND BARRIERS

It's not a question of *whether* something is going to cause you a problem. It's only a question of *what* and *when*. *Make a list of things you can imagine as obstacles on your road to success.* Consider internal and external obstacles. Other barriers may apply to you that we haven't addressed here. Use this three-part system to identify and work through obstacles that stand in the way of career success.

a. Record the potential obstacle.

b. Make a promise that is a solution to the obstacle.

c. Take steps to support the promise.

For example,

a. Obstacle: My tendency to be late.

b. Promise: I'll be on time for all appointments.

c. Steps:
    1) I'll make my car dependable—I'll have it serviced regularly and I'll keep it filled up;

    2) I'll make sure my watch is reliable;

    3) I'll keep a calendar near the toaster so I can review my appointments before my work day begins;

    4) I'll make it a habit to leave fifteen minutes earlier than I need to.

(CONTINUES)

2. Disaster Fantasy Questionnaire

Take on your biggest fear. Maybe it's about a change you want to make or some action you want to take.

a. *Describe the fear or problem:*

b. *Describe what you think could happen* to you as a consequence of the problem:

c. *Record the worst possible outcome:*

d. If the worst happened, *who could you call on for help?*

e. If the worst happened, can you imagine *how you might deceive yourself or sabotage yourself?*

f. If the worst happened, *what positive steps could you take to repair or control the damage?*

g. If the worst happened, *would any of your core values necessarily be compromised?*

h. *What can you do today, before any disaster, to protect yourself from future harm?*

3. Sweep for Bugs

Keep conscious of the potential for sabotage. Don't be paranoid, but don't be naïve, either.

Recruit a Squad of Brand Cheerleaders

You Gotta Have Friends

The road to success is a lot smoother when it's lined with caval-cades of supportive colleagues and zealous mentors to sing your praises, open doors for you, and provide sage advice. Look for guides, teachers, and promoters among your friends, your family, and your colleagues to smooth your path and to help create an atmosphere for success.

Every great brand needs cheerleaders. This is why companies spend millions of dollars on public relations firms, entertainers hire agents and publicists—and career-conscious women look for mentors and coaches to help spread the word about their brands. In fact, we need people whom we can talk to about serious things in *all* areas of living, not just work—friends who may also be business-people, with shared interests and understandings. I have a lot of girlfriends who qualify as my support team—those people I can turn to to build me up in spirit and in word and deed. They are critical to my brand's success.

Emily

Emily can attest to the saving power of cheerleaders. Emily was just forty, just married, and just pregnant, though she hadn't announced this last fact to anyone but her husband. She was a New Yorker born and raised, smart, sharp, competitive, and competent. After earning an undergraduate degree from Princeton, she had moved up the ladder in the financial world with no missteps, starting with Oppenheimer & Co. as a securities analyst in the eighties, moving to Salomon Smith Barney in the nineties, and not long ago changing jobs to accept a directorship at a small institutional brokerage firm on Wall Street. Her goal was a partnership at that firm.

Emily's cheerleaders were a core group of seven other women who had gotten together to create the Manhattan Women's Business Alliance almost a decade ago. They came from all areas of employment. In addition to Emily, one was a travel agent; one owned a gallery/boutique in Tribeca; two were attorneys, one of them a mediation specialist; and there was a marketing executive, the president of a family pharmaceutical laboratory, and a graphic artist. Over the years the alliance had grown to hundreds of professional women, of whom a dozen or more met once a month for lunch at a midtown restaurant, occasionally inviting a guest to speak on some area of interest: the Internet, hiring practices, branding for personal success, and so forth.

The next luncheon was one Emily was not going to miss, and she would ask her group of seven to be there for her, too. She needed all the help she could get. Less than a year since she'd come aboard, the *Wall Street Journal* had reported a rumor that her company had begun merger talks with an online financial service. If it were true, the merger would almost certainly eliminate jobs in both companies. The next day the *New York Times* came out with a similar story, predicting that as many as 40 percent of her company's brokers would be eliminated. Morale at work was somewhere down around zero. While deals needed to be negotiated and the Securities and Exchange Commission would take months to approve any merger, Emily needed a new game plan fast.

"I haven't been there as long as a lot of my colleagues," she told the Alliance when they met. "And I'm pregnant, although nobody knows that yet. The way I see it now, I don't have a chance of being one of the few who keep their jobs—unless I can get an edge on everybody else, do something to really set myself apart and make what I'm offering indispensable to both my company and the merging company."

These were Emily's circumstances. Now let me tell you about the "essential" Emily, whose brand was just about to break out and grab that "edge" she was looking for.

Emily was brainy and ambitious, but one of the things that made her like nobody else was that she was also a fashion junky. Her father was a furrier in Midtown, her grandpa had been a tailor on the Lower East Side, and her great-grandpa had been a tailor, too, so she guessed it was in the genes. She'd rather sit down with a pile of the newest fashion magazines than the latest bestseller. She liked charting fashion trends and following them. She liked watching the industry from a market analyst's point of view, and had used that position to reach out and develop contacts with fashion editors and factory owners—the better to understand the industry. Among the perks of her job were invitations to some of the more prestigious fashion shows. She loved the whole scene, and she didn't want to lose it in somebody else's merger.

Recommendations

Fashion and her knowledge of the fashion industry were Emily's distinguishing characteristics, and her specialty. Now she would have to strengthen her position as one of the *top* analysts in fashion and footwear, and she had to work fast.

The group spent close to two and a half hours focusing their considerable talent and experience on Emily's situation. Everyone agreed that the first thing she needed was a publicist who could pitch her to MSNBC, CNBC, and CNN as the Street's fashion expert. She would say yes to seminars and conventions that she had never really plumbed for what they could offer. And she would solicit invitations to *every* fashion show and event in the United States and abroad, not just the few big ones, to keep her eye on the latest trends, on who was coming up in the ranks and might go public.

Immediately, she would volunteer to write a financial column geared toward women—an untapped market, and yet 51 percent of users—for the company's new Web site.

If Emily is successful in branding herself as one of the leading analysts of fashion and footwear securities, then not only will her firm probably want her to stay after the merger. There's a good chance competing securities firms will be interested in her as well.

Emily's Key Attributes:

- B.A. from Princeton University

- Worked for Oppenheimer & Co. and Salomon Smith Barney

- Known for her fashion sense and un–Wall Street look

- Close contacts with fashion editors and factory owners
- Driven, hardworking, and smart

Emily's Brand Description:

Street-savvy, aggressive, and no-nonsense, Em has got what it takes to be one of Wall Street's leading securities analysts. She's cultivated out-of-the-box research sources, including fashion editors and factory owners to identify trends. Her predictions have been right on, earning her a reputation as one of the hot ones to watch.

Emily's Tagline:

Leading analyst of fashion securities

Learn from the Masters—Attract Mentors Who Matter

Emily's group is clearly a great resource. They'll use their contacts to help her if they can. The marketing executive can put her in touch with a couple of publicists she can choose from, for example. But equally important is the positive reinforcement Emily gets from her peers and their belief that she can succeed, and their willingness to invest their time and energy and more, if necessary, to help her achieve her goal. That's why Step Five in creating a powerful brand is to actively *recruit for support.*

Finding a source of wise opinion and advice,
finding that person who has faith in you,
is like finding an anchor in rough seas.

In every business, there are very successful people who get a genuine thrill out of being able to help someone younger and less experienced than themselves. For them it's payback time for their own good fortune. For you it can be a blessing that one day you'll pass along.

The ideal mentor has made it through many of those principal barriers we've discussed, and can show you the way around them. A mentor will build you up, counsel you, open doors for you, and help you assemble the skills you need to strengthen your brand and succeed. A mentor will speak up for you, put in a good word for you, but mainly teach you the ropes. Learning from a mentor is like learning at the foot of a master. Of all the truly successful people I know, I can't think of anybody who hasn't attributed at least part of his or her success to a mentor. Many people have more than one in their lives, and I'm no exception.

My dad was my first mentor. Sitting with him while he worked, I learned about focusing creative energy. Watching him lay out pages of ads, I learned basic advertising design. Reading his layouts I learned the fundamentals of copywriting. Going with my dad when he pitched a client, I learned that in selling, enthusiasm is contagious. My dad gave me the best possible basics for the career I chose.

When I left my corporate job at Turner and went out on my own, I was incredibly lucky to have one of the most powerful and well-loved men in television become my mentor and pal. I met Brandon Tartikoff through a mutual business associate at one of the many yearly trade shows in my business. Brandon was president of NBC Entertainment in the 1980s, with an amazing, creative intellect, responsible for such classic programming as "Miami Vice," "Cheers," "Hill Street Blues," "The Cosby Show," "Family Ties," and "St. Elsewhere," among others.

"What's the best club in your bag?" he said to me when we were introduced. Thank God my father was an avid golf fan, or I never would have known what he was talking about.

"I make people remember why they got into marketing," I said. "My enthusiasm for promotion is infectious."

"You know, I started in promotions, just like you," he said. "I'll bet you've got some great ideas for TV shows."

Right from the start he challenged me to expand my horizons and think creatively. I didn't really have an idea for TV, but I told him I did. There was no way I was going to pass up this opportunity. I came up with a show concept, and that was the beginning. We'd meet or talk on the phone once a week when he was in town.

"What are you working on?" he'd ask me. "I need to come up with a marketing campaign for ESPN," I'd say. "Great! What have you thought of?" and we'd be off and running, and he'd have a great idea that triggered new ideas for me.

He showed me treatments for proposed shows or pilots for new shows and asked me to tell him what I saw, and he talked to me about what he saw in them. He opened his world to me and introduced me to executives at the highest levels in the entertainment industry. We went together to all the big networks, Fox, CBS, Lifetime TV, to pitch my idea for an animated sit-com targeted at young women. Even though marketing was my first love, playing producer with Brandon was thrilling.

Mentoring relationships usually turn into something else if a sexual component becomes part of it, but it thrives when the relationship is big brother/little sister, or teacher/student. As it progresses, a mentoring relationship can become a true collaboration—Brandon and I talked out ideas and together planned programs and Web sites for the future, and as I was mesmerized by his creative brilliance, I know he was continually energized by my enthusiasm. *The mentor also benefits from his association with you.* But he was clearly my revered teacher in all that we did.

It wasn't all work, it was a mix of business and banter and fun. "What section of the newspaper do you read first?" he asked me—and drew a whole set of conclusions from my answer.

"Say you were abducted by aliens," I said to him, "but they gave you ten minutes to gather together any three things you could take with you. What would you take?" We asked each other these bizarre questions all the time to stay creative.

Brandon Tartikoff died in 1998 when he was forty-eight years old, of complications from Hodgkin's disease. Since then I've met other people he mentored. He was completely generous with his time and really enjoyed taking people under his wing. He was a wonderful, amazing, extraordinary human being, greatly missed.

Finding Your Very Own Brand Guru

People like Brandon are out there, believe me. They may be attracted to a star in the making because they're reminded of themselves starting out, or because they love the role of teacher, or because they have a generous spirit, or all of the above.

Think big and start your search by making an "A" list of people you'd feel lucky to work with and learn from. Add your former bosses and people on your career path who have admired *you* for your innovation, energy, and enthusiasm. Research each prospective mentor as you did your brand audience. Who is this person? Do you have anyone in common with her who could make an introduction? What are her accomplishments? What's the buzz about her? What are her interests? And how can you attract her attention?

To get the ball rolling, simply pick up the phone and start scheduling a few breakfasts or lunches each week with your former bosses and the people you already know. For the people you want to meet, your marketing campaign can consist of a simple engaging, enthusiastic letter explaining that you're looking for a guide and teacher in business and would like the opportunity to discuss that with her, and will call to see if a meeting would be convenient some time next week. Or ask her to lunch and say how much you admire her style and would like to learn from her. A more oblique approach is to target someone you would like to work with, knowing that you'll learn a great deal in the process. Then your charming letter or call would outline your interest in collaboration.

Once the meeting is set, get busy. As in everything, preparation is key. Know in advance how you're going to sell yourself. Review all your best brand qualities. Consult your victory file. Reread your résumé and any articles that have been written about you. Go page by page through your portfolio. If it's appropriate, send some material about yourself ahead of your meeting.

Your prospective mentor will want to know what your goals are so she'll know if she can help you meet them. Be prepared to talk clearly about them. You'll definitely want to explain why you're choosing her in particular as a mentor. In this case, flattery will get you everywhere, but don't overdo it. Base your admiration on her past accomplishments or particular skills. (Obviously, you will have become an expert on your mentor candidate.)

If you're promoting yourself as a collaborator, bring your work proposal with you and be prepared to describe your vision of the project or work involved, how you see working together, and what specifically would be required of each of you.

Be effusive but not cloying in your thanks in the letter you send immediately following your meeting.

If you write and get no response, *be persistent.* If you're turned down, don't necessarily take it to be absolute. Ninety-nine percent of the time you have to pursue your mentor actively. Bhana Grover, specialty CD-ROM producer, age thirty, set her sights on a local businessman who was the founder of an educational toy store chain.[1] She wrote, he didn't answer, she E-mailed, wrote his associates, and wrote again. She sent him a copy of her CDs of Indian fables for children. Eventually he agreed to meet with her. He told her he liked her CDs, but CD-ROMs were not easy start-ups, and he suggested she think about the Internet as her vehicle. He told her she could call him again in a month. When she called again in a month, he agreed to another meeting but not for three months.

Meanwhile, Bhana wasn't just sitting around. She was becoming Internet-savvy.

Her diligence paid off. Her reluctant mentor was knocked out by this persistent, hardworking, passionate entrepreneur and helped her develop her business plan by making her think about and justify every aspect, from the audience she was targeting, to her CDs' content and "look," to her costs and projections. When he was confident that she knew what she was doing and understood every nuance of her venture, her mentor helped her find a half million dollars in venture capital to start up her new company.

Kay's story is similar. She's a mediator, someone who settles disputes between two parties, and one of the seven core members of Emily's Manhattan Women's Alliance. Kay builds her brand by aligning her reputation with the best and brightest legal minds and reputations. She created a list of the ten most respected plaintiff's lawyers in Manhattan, and set out to have each one vouch for her.

She made cold calls to try to set up lunches. These were very busy men and women, and it wasn't easy to get through. But Kay believed that people want to help people, and she persevered. She phoned and wrote and E-mailed. She asked for meetings to introduce herself. She was straightforward about what she wanted: Help getting mediation cases and feedback on how she was handling those cases. Advice on how to move her career forward.

Kay followed up every contact with a note recapping the conversation. She made it easy for these prospects to become mentors by specifying what she wanted and by not wasting their time. She kept herself in front of them, checking in by phone once a week. She attended events where any of these attorneys were speaking. She extended lunch and dinner invitations. Eventually all ten attorneys became Kay-promoters, and the hardest to get became her most valuable supporters. They were flattered by her desire to be coached by them, and they were genuinely in her corner, willing to make a suggestion or open a door, wanting to see her achieve her goals.

Laura

Laura's first mentor was her high school photo teacher, who had taken a special interest in her and her obvious talent, and given her an extracurricular education in slide presentation and project work. Later, in college, studying art education but profoundly affected by her teacher's direction and his passion for the work, Laura took an internship in multimedia as part of her course work.

She interned with a slide show company reputed to be the best in Columbus. Her boss, Joe, taught her how to program a projector to create a moving picture effect, how to use light and color to best advantage, special effects, and all aspects of multimedia presentation for business applications. Much later, after her internship ended, Laura continued to think of Joe as her mentor, although their relationship took a romantic turn and they married. Joe encouraged her to learn the computer aspects of multimedia presentation—something he himself had not done. The mentor was helping the student surpass the mentor.

When Laura took over Samantha's job she had a great deal of technical skill, but with a staff of eight she needed to learn to be a manager. Her company provided a mentor from Human Resources to be her teacher, and they developed a warm and mutually respectful relationship. Laura would ask her for support in her efforts to build her brand within her company.

Mary Beth

Mary Beth had attracted a mentor with her first job at Grey Advertising. One of the art directors there, a fairly outrageous David Bowie look-alike with a vicious wit, in his forties, adored Mary Beth's Carolyn Bessette Kennedy look, her often unusual perspective, and, most importantly, that she laughed at his jokes. He taught her the ropes, and then he encouraged her to apply to Parsons and follow her ambition. She had called him when Grey offered her $50,000 to come back, and he helped her believe it was all right to hold out for something that would make her feel as if every day was full of challenge and promise.

Mary Beth called him again when she was trying to decide about moving to Los Angeles. He turned his Rolodex inside out and provided her with a directory of people to call for everything: help finding an apartment; if all else failed, a job in the art department of Bloomingdale's; a Jungian therapist; and four extremely presentable, very entertaining gentlemen—dear friends of his, two of them artists, two actors—who would be honored to show her the real Hollywood, provide a home-cooked meal, put her in touch with their networks that might be able to help her find what she was looking for, and so forth.

Jillian

Jillian has a very close group of girlfriends she can talk to about her new venture, especially about the emotional aspects, her occasional lapses of confidence, her disappointment over what she perceived as inadequate severance from her previous job. But none of them can offer the kind of business advice she'll need going out on her own in her particular field. Her brand would definitely benefit from the kind of support another professional could give her.

Recommendation

I've recommended that Jillian look for a professional mentor. She had worked with an accountant when she did bookkeeping for the restaurants, and he was someone who might refer clients to her and help her build her business. She would think about approaching him. She might also call SCORE, the Small Business Administration's Service Corps of Retired Executives, which matches its members with your particular industry or needs. They're known especially for mentoring people going out on their own.

The "Let's Work Together" Approach

You can also gain the benefits of mentorship by collaborating with the person you want to learn from. When I started my marketing company, one of the things I did was identify for myself exactly the kind of people I wanted to be working with. Back in 1995 I came across an article about Rick Selvage, who had recently been hired to head up AT&T Interactive, the Internet services arm of AT&T. He was just the kind of person I wanted to know, to work with, and to learn from.

Why Rick Selvage? He was on the cutting edge of the on-line world, which very few people knew anything about. I wanted to be a part of it.

As you know, I'm a strong believer in asking the universe for what I want, so I cut out the article and Mr. Selvage's picture with it, and stuck it in my Daytimer. One day, I thought, we'd work on something together.

Meanwhile, on the theory that the way to get in is to get out, I was meeting people and going to conferences and seminars and attending panel discussions and putting a lot of energy into really selling myself. One of the conferences I went to in L.A. was called Star Power, and one of its panel discussions that I'd come to see was on the future of the Internet in the entertainment industry. Imagine my amazement to look up at the stage—and who should be one of the four panelists but Rick Selvage himself!

At the conclusion of the panel, I ran up to the stage and told him how much I had wanted to meet him, how I was working hard to grow my own company, and how much I wanted to work with him. He clearly liked my enthusiasm, and asked me to write up my thoughts about how we could work together, and send them to him.

The very next day I sent him a proposal for a women's Web site.

But a few days later, before my snail mail had reached him, he called to ask me where my proposal was. When I told him it was in the mail, he chuckled and gave me the first of what would be many important pieces of business advice: "Get E-mail."

You're in the Big Leagues Now

Once you find your mentor, get ready for a wild ride that can enrich you and your brand in a hundred different ways. In today's workplace, gaining the endorsement of a respected mentor is one of the best strategies you can use to move up the proverbial corporate ladder—especially if you can get a top female executive in your company to lower the ladder down to you.

In some cases it's nearly impossible to navigate a company's highly political culture without the help and support of a mentor to guide you through. They protect you from all kinds of principal barriers, most notably competition and saboteurs. They can have you work closely with them, giving you the choice assignments that play to your brand strengths, which will make you shine in the eyes of your superiors.

Connecting with a mentor is like connecting to a higher power than yourself.

The prestige I earned because the legendary Brandon Tartikoff had taken me under his wing was enormous and an incalculable boost to my reputation. People took me seriously (and took my calls!) because I was working with Brandon. And it's more than prestige and opening doors. Being the apprentice means you don't have to learn everything through trial and error. Mentors will steer you away from disaster and share the lessons they learned from their own past mistakes in order to save you having to take the same "hard knocks" they once did. First and foremost, your mentor is your teacher. You should gain knowledge, understanding, and expertise under his or her watch. Mentoring also means there's some-one behind you, rooting for you, a source of positive reinforcement and encouragement.

It's also important that you be a good student—otherwise your mentor will lose interest. Listen to her advice and then put that advice into *action!* Demonstrate that you're not wasting her time and that you appreciate the time she gives you. Your mentor wants you to succeed. If you do, she'll look good, too.

Get on the Mentoring Fast Track

Mentoring is making a comeback in the corporate world in time for the twenty-first century. Many companies today have mentoring programs in place for certain positions. Getting in on one of these programs is a sign that the company considers you fast-track material. Apply for these programs. Ask your immediate supervisor how to go about getting a mentor within the company. You should never leave a job interview without asking the question, "What kind of mentoring program do you have?" Pursue it.

Some companies assign mentors. In some companies you can make direct requests for an individual to be your mentor. Especially in companies where there is no program in place, feel free to solicit a mentor on your own. Look for the person who has the job you'd like to have one day. Look for someone who has qualities you lack and a level of expertise you want to achieve. Look for someone you admire and respect.

There are other places to find mentorship if it isn't part of your company's benefits, and if your overture toward the department head you had hoped would consider you was turned down. (Don't be discouraged if this happens, by the way. Mentoring is a time-intensive commitment and many businesspeople, especially in the higher echelons—and especially women, who are often saving any available extra time for family—regretfully decline to take on a protégée.) Look for private coaches who focus on success in the corporate community, and on-line resources like Coachu.com that offers self-administered questionnaires, a chat room, referrals, questions to ask a prospective coach, and advice on just about anything career-related that you can think of. Or try mentoring.org, which matches its users with your particular industry or need.

Tap into the New Phenomenon of Coaching

Personal business coaching is a hot new trend gaining ground in an increasingly competitive business environment. It makes incredibly good sense to have a seasoned professional "on the payroll" to strategize with you on business moves and hash out your professional concerns. I'm convinced that in the twenty-first century, having a professional business coach will become more commonplace than having a shrink.

My coach, Mariette Edwards, was another fugitive from corporate culture whose former life was as director of human resources for BellSouth. I had regularly scheduled hourlong calls with Mariette twice a week about my business. She counseled me on the fee structure for my consultant services and every other financial aspect of my work, including employees, salaries, bonuses, increasing business, and cutting costs. We discussed improving client relationships and self-promotion. We talked about emotions interfering with the job you're trying to do. You name it, we talked about it.

Mariette was especially valuable for her coaching on how to handle difficult clients effectively. For instance, I had an account with a very important technology company that gave me a lot of work every year, but the head of marketing blatantly displayed his lack of respect by canceling meetings at the last minute and standing me up for business dinners. It got to the point where I truly hated my life any time I had to deal with him. When I confronted him, he apologized profusely and then promised to make it up to me with the carrot of even more business, which he rarely delivered on. It was a prestigious account that I wanted to keep, but how do you do that and stay true to yourself if one of your core values is integrity?

Mariette challenged me to think about whether the business I got from this difficult man was worth the way dealing with him made me feel about myself. In our coaching sessions it became clear to me that no amount of business was worth these negative feelings. I realized I'd probably be no less successful, and certainly a lot happier, if I pursued clients who share my core values. These were the kinds of issues we grappled with.

For our scheduled meetings, I always had a preset agenda so we wouldn't waste any time. (Remember, the clock is running!) Sometimes we did "laser sessions," unscheduled consultations for crisis situations. Mariette made herself available at a moment's notice.

She supported me in holding the empowerment of women as my mission, and she told me that if I wanted to touch many people I needed to learn how to talk to an audience. The idea of public speaking frightened me to death, but her confidence in me helped me push through my fear. She was instrumental in arranging my very first "Brand New You" workshop for a group of one hundred women in the film industry. I told her I wasn't ready, and she said, "I know you're not ready *now*. But you have eight weeks." This is exactly the kind of pressure that makes great leaders out of mere mortals.

Mariette was the first and last person I phoned in any challenging situation. Her cool head and vast experience were invaluable to me as my business grew, and invaluable in my becoming more myself than I had ever been. In this way, she helped me get to know my authentic self, which is really the heart and soul of my brand.

Step 5 Exercises:
Finding a Mentor

Use the strategies below as a checklist for finding a mentor.

1. *Within the company:* Find out about the mentoring program within your company. If there is no program, make a list of individuals you'd like to have as your mentor—someone who has the job you'd like to have, someone who knows what you'd like to learn.

   _____

   _____

   _____

2. *Starting out, or changing careers, or returning to work after time away:* Look for a mentor in the industry you've set your sights on, or in the company you'd like to work for. Look for her in the trade magazines you subscribe to, and at industry conventions. Watch for her during job interviews and while you're researching the firms you apply to. Make a list of prospective mentors.

   _____

   _____

   _____

3. *If you're a consultant, or entrepreneur, or offer a freelance service:* As above, look for someone in your industry who can advise you *and* encourage clients in your direction. List your prospects here.

   _____

   _____

   _____

4. *For all of the above,*

- *Contact the prospective mentor* by letter or E-mail or phone or in person to arrange a meeting.

- *Know your prospect's background.* Maybe you have things in common you didn't know. In any event, this information will automatically help you tailor your letter to suit the audience.

- *Let your prospective mentor know your background,* too, by sending your bio and other pertinent materials to her before your meeting. (Step Seven in this book, Presentation, will be as helpful in attracting a mentor as in attracting your brand audience.)

- *Explain your proposal.* Make the prospect feel as if you'd be worth her time. But don't be cloying or insincere. Since mentoring is a two-way street, be able to explain how your apprenticeship will benefit her.

- *Write a great thank-you letter* after your meeting.

- *Don't take it personally if you're turned down.* Repeat your desires to the universe. Browse through your victory file. Call your support group. Visualize success. Pump yourself up and try again.

- *Consider the professional business coach as mentor.* See what's out there on the Internet and in your community.

- Don't forget the other kinds of support every successful person needs. *Remind yourself of those friends and family members who constitute your board of directors,* your brand advisers, by listing them here:

Learn the Secrets to Packaging Your Brand

ack in the eighties I had a very good friend who was very smart, very charming, and very New York. At my suggestion, he interviewed for an affiliate sales position at Turner Broadcasting when I worked there. After the interview I asked the head of sales who had interviewed him how it had gone. He simply shook his head. "He did two things wrong," he said. "What was that?" I asked. "He wore cufflinks. That's faggy. And I never trust a man in pleated pants. Too slick."

Maybe appearances shouldn't count, and maybe jerks with no sense of style shouldn't be allowed to pass judgments based solely on how someone is dressed, but it happens every day.

*In any business situation,
appearances count, big-time.*

Sure, companies aren't allowed to discriminate against you because of your gender, race, religion, national origin, age, disability, and in most states, sexual orientation, but they certainly *can* decide not to hire you based on your Rasta hair or your multiple piercings. *Packaging is all about appearances and what they signify in the marketplace, and how you can and should use how you look as an integral part of your brand.*

Your Brand-at-a-Glance

First let's be clear: A package is not a mask to disguise the product inside. It's exactly the opposite. It's a way of communicating the essential stuff of the product at a glance. If a product is a trusted brand, a customer will toss it in the shopping cart without a thought. But if it's brand-new, if she notices it at all, she's likely to look at the package and be positively—or negatively—influenced by everything that went into designing it: the shape of its box, its graphics, colors, typeface, and so forth. The package is a powerful tool that, if used correctly, can influence a customer to buy.

When I talk about packaging yourself as a brand, the exact same rules apply. Your audience is going to be consciously and unconsciously influenced by your appearance, and this includes your shape and size and the way you dress—basically all your physical attributes and accessories, all the outerwear. You'll also be evaluated on what your business card looks like, by the stationery you use, by your résumé or portfolio, by your outgoing voicemail message, and your Web site. All these are parts of your package.

> *Your challenge is twofold: to make your exterior appealing to your target audience, and to make sure your exterior is as much a genuine reflection of your interior as possible.*

But what if the *real* you is most comfortable in ripped jeans and an old sweatshirt? What if your passion is the great outdoors, and your authentic self is best expressed in hiking gear? Or what if you're essentially a sex kitten who feels happiest in plunging necklines and stretch fabrics?

Well, get a grip. We're talking about your professional life, not your leisure life and definitely not your sex life. Most of the world accepts that the clothes you wear to work aren't the same ones you wear on a date. We're talking about authenticity within the realm of what's acceptable in your particular business culture. You may push the edges of what's acceptable, and in some creative jobs, you absolutely should push the edges. But it's rarely productive to break too far out of your business culture's comfort zone. If you do you'll probably be branded "inappropriate" or "uninformed."

The very best packages, the ones imprinted on our minds eternally, are completely consistent with their product's own unique qualities.

Colonel Sanders wants you to know that you get a *lot* of chicken at Kentucky Fried Chicken. What better package could he have invented than a bucket? Apple computer has always been the definitive alternative to the PC, but for most of the nineties it came in the same drab nondescript beige box as its competitors and it wasn't selling a whole lot of product. The Mac simply wasn't hot anymore. But all that changed with the introduction of the iMac. Sleek, futuristic, and downright cute, the iMac even offered six vibrant colors to choose from. All of a sudden, the computer that had built its reputation on being fun and easy to use was back, its very look reminding people of fun (those colors!) and how easy it is to use (it's all one piece).

Here's another example of a product that communicates much about its inner qualities in its packaging: The venerable Quaker Oats box in its familiar cylinder is a heavier cardboard than other cereal boxes. This suggests to consumers that what's inside the package is also "heavier," or of superior quality. Years ago many families kept their empty Quaker Oats boxes as storage containers, which added the concept of utilitarianism to the brand and tied in perfectly with the Quaker image on the label, communicating that eating Quaker Oats is an act of prudence and even piety. In the 1940s, when Tinker Toys entered the marketplace, its box was also a fat cylindrical shape, and Quaker benefited from this further subliminal association with one of the bestselling children's toys pre-1975.

Just as Apple and Quaker Oats tell their customers about their key attributes through packaging, you want your outerwrap to say something true about your unique qualities and attributes.

Head to toe, your package should express
your creative energy, your talent, your warmth,
your way of thinking, your expertise—all those non-
physical, inner attributes, the qualities that
in combination make you like no other.

It's that unique combination of your own best qualities that your package has to put across—not only when you're there in person, but when you're not there. When your prospective employer goes to your Web site, say, or when you've sent a letter or left your card or dropped off your video or résumé or portfolio to his or her attention, you want those accessories that you use in your professional life to speak clearly and even elegantly about who you are.

Pizza or Tuna Tartare?
Consider Your Audience's Tastes

What does your audience want to see? What kind of package does it respond to, feel safe with, understand, respect, admire? What kind of package can you put together to motivate, or even *excite,* your audience?

Conduct your own market research to find out what your target audience finds attractive, reassuring, nonthreatening, "professional," or cool; and this will be different for different markets. If I were interested in working with the FBI, I would definitely go for a different look than the one I'm comfortable wearing in the TV and Internet field.

How do you find out what works for your audience? Look at

how they package themselves. Yes, I'm talking about walking through the lobby of the building where you'll be interviewing or meeting a prospective new client next week. Why not? This job is important to you.

Show up a little after noon or one o'clock when people are leaving for lunch so you get to see lots of people coming and going, and they're not as liable to notice you observing because they're focused on lunch. If you show up in a conservative suit and find everyone there dressed in jeans (and it's not a casual Friday), you might want to reconsider what you were planning to wear to the meeting. If you discover that nearly everyone's dressed in solids or black, you'll want to rethink wearing that pony print jacket.

What if you're going to work for a small firm, or for someone who's self-employed or works out of her home? My office is in a separate building on our property. You could try hanging out on my corner at lunchtime but you wouldn't see much action: mothers and strollers, nice houses, serene landscaping. Forget about the "research" method described above. But it doesn't take a rocket scientist to get that we don't require corporate attire. So I was surprised recently when I interviewed several women for the job of marketing coordinator at my company, and two of them arrived in navy blue skirts and bow-tie blouses.

News flash: The generic "dress for success" look went out in the eighties.

Dressing for success today means reflecting your authentic self in a way that attracts your target audience.

Maybe these two job applicants were authentically bow-tie-type people, very "buttoned up." Still they could have demonstrated their personal modesty without looking as if they were stuck in a time warp.

How could they have known what to wear? Well, they might have asked around. In the course of preparing for their interview with me they should have found out something about me and my company and the kind of work we do. In other words, they should have studied my brand, which is certainly out there for all to see. If they had, they would have gotten the idea that we are an innovative, cutting-edge organization. They might have gathered that style is important to us, and that creativity is one of our key interests.

The fact that these two women showed up looking wrong for the job told me a lot: that they hadn't done their homework about my company, and that in spite of impressive résumés and references they weren't especially creative or hip, both important qualities for the position I was looking to fill.

Distinguish yourself from your competition and
the rest of the crowd, but don't look so out of sync
as to give the impression you'd never fit in.

There's security in looking like the other successful brands in your category. That's why almost every brand of baking soda comes in an orange box, trying to look as much like the big guy, Arm & Hammer, as possible. It's why most salt is packaged in a cylindrical box to look like Morton's, and why Gold Medal and Pillsbury flour are both in similar looking bags. It's not necessarily an effort to confuse consumers. More likely it's a way to reassure. Finding that place where you look just right, but are distinguished from everyone else, is how you win awards for packaging.

Clothes: Establish a Signature Style That's Memorable

Most traditional cultures are distinguished by their dress. What a culture wears tells you something about the way its people live. When you think of Eskimos you get a mental image very specific to dress. You can identify whole populations by certain garments: the sari, the kimono, the chador—the three-piece suit and power tie.

Once your market research has revealed the culture of the industry you're targeting, you'll want to study that culture's dress as if you were an anthropologist. Your brand wants to reassure its audience by the way it looks and at the same time demonstrate some of its best characteristics. Neatness, a sense of style, understatement, can communicate something about your work habits, your hip quotient, and your personality. So can being unbuttoned or untucked, or demonstrating overt sexiness, communicate inattention and sloppiness, and even leave negative impressions about your morals.

If you're in marketing or advertising, if you're an artist or musician or inventor, a designer or architect, or someone in the fashion industry, or in writing or editing, or entertainment, or any other industry in which your creative credibility is important, it's imperative that you communicate something about your creativity in the style of your dress.

How I Lassoed AOL

I was on my way up in the elevator, trying to concentrate on the progress of the illuminated numbers above the door, and not on the man standing directly across from me. This guy was not even trying to be discreet about looking me up and down. It's not that I didn't want to be noticed. I was wearing a brown riding jacket and pants, and a man's tie boldly printed with a cowboy busting a bronco. But given the reaction, I thought maybe this time I'd gone too far in my effort to brand myself as creative and edgy.

Finally the doors opened and we both turned in the same direction, toward Brandon Tartikoff's office. Now I was really uncomfortable.

We sat down in the outside waiting room and he looked at me again. "From the way you're dressed," he said, "I can tell you must be creative. What do you do?"

It was exactly the response I wanted, but boy, was I surprised to hear him say it! I told him all about my company and the kinds of clients we had and the kinds of projects we did. Then I asked him, "What do you do?"

"I'm Charlie Fink," he said. "I head up America Online's Greenhouse, the R&D area of the company," he said.

And guess what? He was looking for a creative hand in branding and developing proposals and presentations for three new Web sites: one for women, one for entertainment, and one a matchmaking site. America Online became my client that day—a major enhancement to my portfolio and résumé—owing largely to my wearing my creativity on my sleeve!

But if your work is in a conservative industry like banking or finance, insurance, sales, real estate, human resources, science, medicine, research, academia, the law, politics, civil service, social work, counseling, and even the administrative and organizational arms of all those "creative" fields mentioned above, you're going to want to package yourself to complement your industry's standard. But you should always look current and stylish to the degree that's acceptable in your field and in your environment, no matter what you do for a living.

You don't want to copy anyone, and above all, it's important to wear what feels good on you. If you're not comfortable with your package, if it chafes, or pulls, or hangs wrong, if it makes you feel self-conscious for any reason—because it's shorter than you're used to wearing, or tighter than you usually wear, or a color you're unaccustomed to—it's the wrong package. When you find the right package, you'll know it. You'll feel comfortable, fashionable, and attractive, a combination that makes you feel competent, secure, and savvy. Your self-confidence soars when you've got your packaging right.

Mary Beth

More than anything else, black and white defines Mary Beth's signature style. She likes crisp white stretch cotton shirts with three-quarter sleeves and slim black trousers with a flat front. She thinks her tangerine Mac ibook is her best accessory. "That and my Palm Pilot." She wears her shoulder-length blond hair pulled back in a sleek ponytail or with a skinny headband. She likes chunky loafers, and wears a Cartier tank watch that her dad gave her when she graduated from Emory. Banana Republic is her best bet on a budget, and she doesn't hesitate to order clothes off the Web.

I like Mary Beth's choice of black and white. It's another way her brand says "I'm different." And I think it's great that her ibook is her one jolt of color because it draws attention to her medium and says, "Here's where I generate the real excitement!"

Jillian

Jillian reminds you of Jacqueline Kennedy Onassis, in her style, her quiet elegance, and even in her looks. She's dark-haired with a touch of gray, slim, and very pretty. And like Jackie, clothes are one of her passions. Because she has great taste she can have an extensive wardrobe, and with a few notable exceptions, not spend a fortune on it. Jillian wears earth tones, ivory, and mossy colors mixed with black. When she's meeting a client she often wears a lower calf-length skirt or the new knee-lengths in a good fabric with high black leather boots or slingbacks, a great matching jacket, often with a wonderfully textured scarf. She uses minimal makeup and glossy natural-colored lipsticks.

The length of the skirts and simplicity of her makeup suit Jillian and communicate a professional who's not frivolous, but is stylish.

Laura

Laura is short and full-figured and wears slim cropped pants, solid-color sweater sets in cashmere or 100-percent cotton, and hip-length jackets that complement rather than overwhelm her petite physique. She believes that having a few very fine pieces of clothing is better than a closet full of mediocre outfits. Laura dresses for comfort because she's at the computer most days, and wears low-heeled pumps or square-toed black boots. She chooses pant suits for meetings with CEOs, sticking to grays and black but accessorizing with fabulous silk scarves in animal prints or shot with color. She wears her brown, straight hair short and cut into a smart bob.

Laura is going to speak to a makeup consultant to "upgrade" her look with a subtle makeover that adds the impression of polish and professionalism. With this year's bonus, she'll treat herself to a good watch and a pair of real pearl earrings.

Emily

The quintessential New York fashion hound, Emily clears the rack at Barney's semi-annual sale to snap up designer clothes. Small, funky frames are Emily's signature look, which she changes almost daily to match her outfits. She carries a Kate Spade tote, and wears her dark hair cropped super-short, one-carat diamond studs, a stainless steel man's diving watch, bright red lipstick and no other makeup.

She's got her eye on her husband's dress shirts for later in her pregnancy and will have panels sewn into her slacks to accommodate her growing tummy.

Emily's package says "Wall Street meets Seventh Avenue." It's perfectly suited to her brand.

Seven Brand Fashion Essentials

To discover your personal taste, cut out pictures in fashion magazines that are expressive of your brand and convey something about your personal attributes. Then make a collage of what you find attractive. This is a great first step to building your brand on the outside. In this exercise, you'll try to create a unique, professional fashion statement that you think will be noticed and accepted by your audience—your business culture. You might include a fabulous pair of Kenneth Cole shoes, colors that speak to you, hair styles, sweaters, slacks, jackets, skirts, jewelry, lipsticks, nails—fill an $11^1/_2$ × 17–inch piece of poster board with fashion elements that you can take to work.

What colors appeal to you most? Is your palette vivid or muted, is the jewelry gold or silver, are the lengths long or short? Could you ever pull off something as form-fitting as that gray long-sleeved woolen jersey, or do you think you need to go back to the gym? Do you lean toward the no-nonsense, very tailored look, or is a tiny bit of whimsy more your style? Do the models in your piece of art look like mannequins, are they coiffed and polished, or are they more "natural" looking? Bring your finished collage to your hairdresser, your favorite store, or your personal shopper. If you're your own hairdresser and shopper, use this fashion palette as a guide for developing a personal style. Carry it with you when you shop.

Beyond your personal taste, you are looking for a seamless "wrapping" for your brand. Now ask yourself how this wrapping compares with the way the people in your profession actually dress and look. If there's a wide divide, you're going to have to regroup. You may not be able to wear that hot pink sweater set to Wall Street, but no one will fault you a hot pink barrette, or clipboard, or mousepad.

1. THE EVERY-BRAND ENSEMBLE: Do spend money on one good white blouse with cuffs, a well-tailored black pants suit (dark

colors convey authority), a print scarf, a top-notch handbag, great shoes, and a good watch. These are the essentials for any corporate-type business—though there's some question about the handbag. Madeleine Albright stopped carrying a purse when she became Secretary of State. Her feeling was that the handbag diminished her credibility as a person of power. She put one of her Secret Service men in charge of holding whatever she might otherwise use a purse for.

Ever since I heard this about Madeleine Albright, I've noticed that you rarely see other women in politics with a purse anymore, the Queen of England being an exception. If you do decide to stash the purse, use a Secret Service man, or a fabulous briefcase or portfolio into which you can toss a bag that contains personal necessities.

2. TERRIFIC TAILORING: Take a tip from the CEOs of big businesses. Always tailor your clothes to fit beautifully.

3. SOLEFUL STYLE: Keep your shoes resoled. Uneven heels are signs of disrepair. They communicate someone who's down and out, not up and coming. And along the same lines, a run in your hose is like a rip in the package. No one will buy it.

4. CHEAP CHIC: If you can't afford new clothes, buy vintage. Raid your grandmother's or mother's closet for treasures. If your company's culture is conservative or classical, shop at a consignment store where you're likely to find high-quality, more conservative, classic-style, once-pricey items.

5. COOL GLASSES: If you wear glasses, buy a new pair every year or so. Staying contemporary is an important part of brand strategy, and what you wear on your face (and this includes makeup) says something about how current you are in your thinking.

6. UPDATE OR DIE: Get a free professional makeover at your local department store to update your look in spring and fall. If your

budget doesn't allow for the luxury of a whole new bag of makeup when the seasons change, a single tube of lipstick in a new shade can be enough to make you look and feel brand-new.

7. THE SIGNATURE PIECE: Find a signature piece or develop a signature "look." Sharon Stone stands out with her fabulous, short blond cut. Isabella Rossellini has cupid lips. If you're not comfortable highlighting physical attributes like these, choose an accessory or a style marker and make it your own. For instance, early in her career in the late sixties and early seventies, you never saw Cher except in bell-bottoms. (She got married to Sonny in bell-bottoms.) They said, "I'm kicky, I'm unconventional, I'm modern!"

The writer Tom Wolfe is known for his white suits. Frank Lloyd Wright wore a long, swinging cape. Larry King wears suspenders and often a bow tie. They say, "I'm not your typical talk-show host, but I am consistent." Sally Jessy Raphael's red-framed glasses are part of her package. They read "serious" and "feisty" at the same time. Lady Di wore gorgeous hats that communicated "regal."

I have a friend who's an engineer for Sony who wears a square computer chip lapel pin. I know an actress who wears the masks of comedy and tragedy in a gold and silver ring. You could make your signature piece an heirloom pin, your grandfather's watch, a classic alligator Kelly bag, or a great belt with a Western silver and turquoise buckle. These things give people an opening to talk with you—they are "recognizers."

Four Fashion Divas

What you're trying to do is establish a look that's absolutely you and that absolutely works in your work. Look for role models in your industry. Try to figure out how their outerwear puts their inner selves across. For example:

Diane Sawyer, the first woman correspondent for CBS's "60 Minutes," is a style icon and anchor for current-events type shows, lately "Primetime Live" and "Good Morning America." She has to look attractive, but also serious and credible. She has to appeal to men and women, blue collar and white collar, yet reflect a hint of glamour.

Diane Sawyer was America's Junior Miss when she was seventeen years old. Today she still retains the essence of an all-American, unspoiled, girl-next-door. She pulls this off by wearing up-to-the-minute makeup for *a very natural look,* a gorgeous blond cropped hairstyle that isn't especially sexy but is extremely flattering, and very *simply cut, well tailored suits in flattering pastels that communicate femininity, or dark solids that express authority.* She made *People* magazine's "Ten Best Dressed" list in 1999. She always looks fresh, clean, and totally appropriate.

She appears confident and at the same time modest and non-threatening. She dresses that way.

Carolyn Bessette Kennedy, a private reserve brand. There was a *pristine* quality and a youthful *elegance* to her look, communicated in the *austerity and simplicity of her dress,* whether in jeans playing Frisbee in Central Park, in a bathing suit at Hyannisport, or attending a fashionable New York black-tie event in a simple silky sheath. Clean, all-American, and at the same time regal, she wore a plain wedding band and no other jewelry. That itself said volumes about what she valued.

Candice Carpenter, CEO of iVillage, a wildly popular Internet site for women, is an entrepreneur and media mogul. When I asked her about her unique style, she confessed that after leaving her corporate job, she couldn't wait to become a diva. I met the slim, attractive forty-seven-year-old Carpenter at a Women & Co. conference. She used minimal makeup, her *romantic Rapunzel hair* was loose, and she wore a fabulous *pink cropped* *pantsuit with gorgeous mules and fun tortoiseshell glasses.* Her *best accessory of all was her three-year-old daughter,* who held her hand, looking smart and cool in a dress and her own little round glasses. Candice couldn't have looked more brand-perfect for someone *dedicated to providing a resource for women to help balance their lives.* She's not afraid to look like a woman or act like one, and so she actually personifies her target audience's aspirational self.

Cher's great packaging has contributed to the strength of her brand for over forty years and counting. She's as much a personality as a singer and actress. She's kept her body beautiful in order to indulge her *passion for costume,* which is as much a comment on our times as on her cutting-edge taste. From the bell-bottom jeans and sheepskin vests of the sixties to the lanky, long skirts and bare midriff of the seventies, from the spandex skin-tight, cut-out looks of the eighties to today's perfectly groomed, polished Cher, she always shows us how what's hot can sizzle. Cher is *a brand that lasts.* She's probably good for another forty years.

How to Outwardly Express Your Brand's Attributes

Your clothes and makeup are the first things that come to mind when we think of packaging for people, but there are other aspects of your package that are also worth a thousand words.

Wheels

Your car is the package you arrive in. My workshop participant who called herself "the ultimate driving machine" may not drive a BMW herself, but it would be a brand-breaker if she showed up in a junker littered with beer cans.

Pierre Mornell, who checks out prospective hires for big companies, likes to walk candidates back out to their car after his interviews. "Cars tell a lot about a person," he writes in *Hiring Smart!*

> "Once I met a rather odd candidate who arrived late to our interview. He was a prospect for the sales manager's job at a chain of retail stores. Afterward, we walked to the man's car, which was parked at an angle to the curb and stuffed with clutter, clothes, tools, and newspapers piled up to the windows. As dogs sometimes look like their owners, so did this man's car look like him. . . .
>
> "My biggest surprise walking a candidate to his car was when I discovered the candidate's wife sitting inside the automobile waiting for him. She and her husband knew our interview was to last two hours. Why wasn't she in my waiting room? Why didn't the candidate suggest a soft drink from my kitchen? . . . Two hours in a hot car on a warm August day said more about the candidate than any of my questions in the interview."[1]

Mary Beth

When Mary Beth moves to Los Angeles, she'll buy herself a new VW bug. It's original and youthful and winks at you from the road. She'll choose silver from the wide range of colors, sensing that the metallic color will convey richness and somehow ground the whimsical look of the car.

Laura

Laura drives a red minivan. It says, "I'm a mom first." Her next car will be a black Explorer for a little edgier look that's kid-friendly but communicates a somewhat higher level of sophistication. Laura isn't *only* trying to create an impression at work. She's also interested in developing an edgier, more sophisticated persona for *herself*.

The Résumé

Think of your written or visual support material, your résumé, portfolio, or brochure as if it were part of your brand's ad campaign. You'll want it to feature your work history, but to set yourself apart you'll need more. You also want to zap your reader with who you are, with your greatest attributes. You want your brand's core values and unique expertise to shine through your résumé.

Look at any of Paul Newman's "Newman's Own"–brand products. His Venetian Pasta Sauce, for instance, lists nutrition facts along with its "all natural" ingredients, but it also sports this "legend" on the label that purports to describe how the actor invented the product:

> **Legend:** Working 12-hour days . . . wrecked . . . hungry . . . arrive home, deserted by wife and children . . . cursing! Scan the cupboard—one package spaghetti . . . one bottle marinara sauce . . . run to the kitchen, cook—junk! YUK! Lie down, snooze . . . visions of culinary delights . . . Venetian ancestor tickles my ear, tickle, tickle . . . sauce talk . . . MAMA MIA! Dash to the vegetable patch . . . Yum yum . . . boil water . . . activate spaghetti . . . ditto the sauce . . . slurp, slurp . . . Terrifico! Magnifico! Slurp! Caramba! . . . Bottle the sauce! . . . share with guys on streetcar . . . ah, me, finally immortal![2]

True story or not, it's good-natured, it's wild, it's a little crazy. It makes a statement. The statement is: This is different! But the jar looks like most of the other clear glass jars on the grocer's shelf, and the sauce looks pretty much like every other tomato sauce on the shelf, so we're reassured that the product isn't going to be too wild and crazy and will probably taste like what we're used to. May be better.

There's also an oval on the label that proclaims, "Paul Newman gives all profits to charity . . . (over $100 million since 1982)," which says something very important about Newman's Own brand values.

The label also offers visual clues to help influence a shopper: Paul Newman's broadly smiling face, the centerpiece for a bouquet of fresh flowering herbs and plump vegetables and a tangle of spaghetti says that he has a sense of humor, and that this is "fun" food, but he also lets us know with the words "all natural" that it's wholesome, good-for-you food.

So in addition to the specifics of your previous work life, which we can compare to the nutritional facts and ingredients on your label, you want your résumé or your catalogue or brochure to speak in your voice and to communicate something about who you are and what your values are.

Your previous retail work may be less important than your personality, enthusiasm, dedication, and desire to be Macy's best floor manager. Your lack of experience in marketing may count less than your phenomenal knack for taking the pulse of the next generation of consumers. That's what you've got to get across in a single page.

Consider doing these things to allow your personality to shine through:

- Include your mission statement. It's fairly common to announce your "objective" in applying for a new position. It's less usual for people to share the deeper statement of their personal ambition.

- Include your brand's best qualities. Feature your key attributes, using examples from your professional life. You might use these as subsections in your résumé. For instance:

Key Attribute: Creative Thinking

In the summer of 1987, as promotional director for Z93, Atlanta's hot top-40 rock station, I directed and produced a $25,000 Scavenger Hunt. We announced one item a day for twenty-five days. The city went berserk.

One of the items we asked for was a signed picture of David Letterman. He was deluged with calls and even mentioned our station and our promotion during his show. So many people participated that we had to hold the collection site in the middle of a big shopping mall. Every TV station showed up. It was a huge success.

This benefit-driven statement shows the kind of work I did then, and provides details, but it's different than the usual boring chronological list of past jobs, and it's written as if I'm telling a story, not reciting a litany, which makes it much nicer for the person stuck with reading these things that usually all sound pretty much the same.

Along with your résumé, another opportunity to push your brand's uniqueness is in your cover letter, a concise, yet warm introductory note that relates specifically to the job you're interested in, and those key attributes that you'll bring to the job when you're hired on (which you may have featured in the résumé itself). The cover letter is how you personalize your résumé for the work you're looking to find. Consult any of the zillions of how-to-write-a-brilliant-résumé-and-cover-letter books and adapt their suggestions to the ones included here.

- Close your résumé with a Closing Comments or P.S. or Other Amazing Facts that will allow the reader to get a feel for the real you. Mention that you volunteer at the Food Closet, play the bagpipe, have won a short story writing contest, whatever. Make your writing personable, not stiff and formal, and see what happens. If you're not a writer, and can't pull off a document that adequately reflects something of your authentic self in addition to your work history, then hire someone to help you with this aspect of your package. It's every bit as important as what you wear to your interview.

Mary Beth

When Mary Beth revised her résumé to reposition herself for the Internet, she added this closing comment: Fluent in French, Spanish, and HTML.

Stationery/Business Cards/Logo

When I left Turner Broadcasting I cashed out my Turner stock—$10,000 worth—to start my marketing business, which I called Big Fish Marketing. Of the $10,000, I spent $3,000 to print stationery and business cards. That's how important I think they are. And the investment has been priceless. A cherished friend of mine *gave* me the gift of my logo. My friend, who I knew was a genius, said, "I'm going to do your logo, but I'm only going to show you one piece of art and that's the art you're going to take." He was obviously psychic, too, because he came back about a week later with my dream logo—a wonderful, stylized "big fish" with a great expression, in a plump, flat, wicker market basket. It says, "I only work with the big fish, and I know how to catch them and bring them to market." I wouldn't have changed a thing.

I don't even have to use my company name anymore—the logo says Big Fish Marketing without the words, and by now it has instant recognition in my industry. I've used it in a dozen different ways, including having hand-carved wooden mobiles made of it, and Egyptian cotton pillow cases printed with it, and fluffy cotton bathrobes embroidered with it for gifts—all things that say "quality."

Look at color, look at typefaces. Flip through cutting-edge magazines. Look at what's prominent in advertisements, in clothing, in print. Check out *Vogue, Wired,* and *Metropolitan Home* to anticipate trends you can build on. I actually went to a former Wall Street analyst-turned-business-astrologer with my Big Fish logo to ask her what colors would appeal to people in the 1990s and into the next century. She thought the Pisces image was great for my company, and advised me that green and blue were going to be the colors of the nineties. "They're the colors of grass and sky, and they'll dominate as we continue to be concerned with our planet's environmental health."

You may not require a graphic logo. You may use your name and tagline only for business cards, or your name alone on note paper or stationery. I feel very strongly about good paper. I think it shouts quality and credibility. Mine is very smooth and heavy—twenty-four-pound bond with a watermark.

And what typeface will you choose? Make sure it reflects the personality of your brand in a way that says bold, classic, contemporary, hip, whatever is truest of you.

There's a lot to consider, and a lot of intuitive, what-feels-right that has to go into deciding. You may not want to consult an astrologer, but ask for plenty of feedback from family, friends, and colleagues who have taste and "get" your brand. Look at what other people in your field use and figure out how to stand out from the pack. Ask your coach. Talk to your mentor. Don't rush into a decision. For consistency's sake as well as economical sense, you want your stationery and business cards to last.

The Self-Promotional Book or Portfolio or Brochure

Artists, photographers, architects, and designers carry a portfolio, often an oversized book with a zippered leather cover. Don't chintz out when it comes to the show-and-tell props you need to sell your brand. Proudly present your work in a great leather binder, a sleek silver case, or an interesting wooden box.

Recently I read about a literary agent who sent a book proposal around to a half-dozen publishers in a pizza box (to keep it hot). I've heard of cookbooks going out to reviewers with fresh-baked samples of some of the recipes.

I have a friend who's a landscape artist whose brochure leads with a photo of herself standing in a waist-high field of wheat, with the caption, "Deanna Boer, Outstanding in Her Field." Inside, the brochure describes the kind of services she offers and lists some of her clients. Carol Costello is the "book doctor" whose clever brochure plays off the kinds of "treatments" she offers manuscripts.

My company's current brochure uses the image of a woman standing in ankle-deep water on the edge of a lake, with a fly rod in her hand and a wicker basket slung over one shoulder. Her back is to us, but you can tell by her hairstyle, by her thigh-length shorts and short-sleeved shirt with shoulder pads, and by the wristwatch she wears that the photo is an old one, 1940s or early fifties. We've colored it with a sort of blue-green-purple tint that looks a little like sepia and a little like sunlight refracted on the surface of water. In silver letters that make you think of a silver fish, we've written, "HOOK, Line & Sinker."

Inside the brochure, we promise "We'll Reel in Your Brand," and we reinforce that promise with an explanation of our expertise, our capabilities, and a client list. (My fish-in-the-basket logo makes its appearance inside, too.)

I consider this brochure to be an important piece of my company's packaging. It echoes my other package pieces, my stationery and business cards, and it carries my logo. Its 1940s image and the sepia-like tint we use is retro, which is very "in" right now. (Notice the return of the Jolly Green Giant, Mr. Peanut, Mr. Whipple, and other characters from bygone days.) Our use of nostalgia tells people that we're in tune with what's hot, and we still value what's classic. The choice of colors was purposeful: silver is associated with money, and the water motif is calming and inviting to a busy executive who receives the piece during a meeting-filled day.

Inside, our capabilities and client lists are bullet-pointed for a quick read. Our contact info is bold, not buried. We used a heavy card stock to communicate value. Custom-made mailing envelopes with our return address embossed on the back make the piece look like an invitation, not like a piece of junk mail. And we used a beautiful stamp. Forget postage machines!

Your Work Environment

As much a part of your wardrobe as your power suit, your immediate work environment should be considered part of your package, whether it's a desk among many in a large open room, or a cubicle, or an office of your own, or a room in your home. A desk whose surface isn't visible and is piled with files, loose paper, last week's newspapers, or an assortment of nail polishes or empty coffee containers communicates something about your brand that you may not have intended.

On the other hand, a barren landscape in your work space also says something. Demonstrate to your colleagues that you have a life. Hang well-framed pictures in your office, stand an artifact from your travels on your bookcase, install a fabulous area rug, a decorative wall clock, artwork that reflects your taste.

I have two favorite female executive offices. One is a publisher's in a big New York office building. It would have to be called totally shabby-chic: antique white furniture, overstuffed sofas with flouncy slipcovers—very country French, very feminine and romantic. It even has a chandelier! This executive editor handles mostly women's books, and you can tell when you walk in that she's fine-tuned to what's comfortable and appealing to women. My other favorite office is in a movie studio, upholstered with animal prints, filled with fabulous artifacts from faraway places, an inlaid armoire from Bali, a family of wooden giraffes from Africa. The feeling in this room is very Ralph Lauren safari—and the executive is a tiger! Both work environments say, "I'm like nobody you ever met before—and I'm in charge!"

Your Web site

If you're one of the nearly twelve million women among the working ranks who are self-employed, a Web site is a very powerful tool for further establishing your brand identity and your business. It's also a great way for individuals to distinguish themselves within a corporate system. Mieko is a programmer at a well-known Silicon Valley company, whose personal Web site includes a "career highlights" link, basically excerpts from her résumé; a "personal history" link for the heartwarming story of the small-town girl who sought her fortune in the big city; reviews of movies she's seen recently; favorite recipes; and a column, updated weekly, on a variety of subjects, from her kitty, Buster's, latest antics, to her thoughts on gun control. The columns, often no more than a page long, have become "must reads" among her colleagues and supervisors. Everybody at her large company knows her name—she's a bookmark on about five hundred computers in Palo Alto, California. Her colleagues all know what's important to her, and her on-line talents, sense of design, and ability to express herself are obvious to anyone who accesses her page—and she averages fifty hits a day. When she's introduced, eyes light up.

Think of your Web site as a personal scrapbook to share within the professional community. Think of it as another kind of package and be as attentive to its composition, color, layout, typeface, and so forth as you are to your résumé or your portfolio. Then when you go in for your interview, bring your laptop with you, plug in, and log on.

Get a lot of input on your Web site before you launch it. Does it seem like you? Is it interesting? Visit other personal Web sites to see what they look like and what works and what doesn't. Vow to keep your Web site fresh, updating information, adding links, retiring others.

Step 6 Exercises:
Brand Packaging

Observe what colors people are wearing in your business culture. What length skirts? What kind of jewelry, what hair lengths and styles, what level of makeup, fingernail polish or not, casual shoes or sexy heels? Create a collage that will reveal your brand's packaging preferences. Compare to your business culture. If you're on the same page, use the collage for ideas when you appraise your closet at home and while you shop.

Use the list of items below for this kind of review, and add items appropriate to your particular situation—any of the outerwear that can be considered part of your brand's package. What kind of shape is your package in? Make color notes. Does any item in your wardrobe need repair or replacing? Make a note here.

1. CLOTHES

Your game suit, appropriate to your corporate culture, your audience, your clientele, or your marketplace, may include the following:

- shoes
- dresses
- skirts
- slacks
- suit
- blouses
- sweaters
- jackets
- coat
- stockings/socks

2. HAIR

(CONTINUES)

3. Cosmetics

4. Nails

5. Fragrance

6. Dress accessories

- jewelry
- handbag
- briefcase/portfolio
- hats
- scarves
- gloves
- signature piece
- belts

7. Professional accessories

- resume/portfolio/brochure
- business cards/stationery

8. Car

9. Office/work space

- neatness counts
- demonstrate that your brand is multidimensional

10. Web site

- list various areas you'll invite visitors to explore
- don't forget to personalize and update

Get Comfortable in Your Own Skin

ack in my Turner days, when it seemed like a new channel was launching almost daily, we brought on a lot of new people. I asked my boss what criteria he was using, apart from experience, to make hiring decisions. He told me he was looking for folks "that I'd enjoy having a drink with." What was most important to him was being comfortable with the people he brought on board.

It's easy to draw others in and make them feel comfortable when you're comfortable with yourself. This kind of inner comfort comes from the inner knowledge that you're okay just the way you are. Women are too often apologetic for their shortcomings, when we should be accepting, even celebrating ourselves, warts and all.

So you're flawed. Who isn't? Barbra Streisand has a reputation for being "difficult"; Camryn Manheim, of TV's *The Practice,* is a big woman with a robust figure; Barbara Walters can't pronounce the letter "R." But each of these superstars has become comfortable with what might be considered her "flaw" and turned it into one of her unique characteristics, and therefore an important feature of her brand.

Cultivating a personal style is what Step Seven is all about. You start by identifying your personality/attitude, you become completely comfortable and accepting of your style markers, and then you fully integrate them into your brand strategy.

Shining a Light on Your Dark Side

I remember my father telling me when I was a teenager, "Kid, life isn't all peaches, cream, and honey. You've got to learn to grow a thick layer of skin."

Let's face it, there are people out there who are very comfortable expressing their dark side to you without regret. The ones at the top—and in my experience, that's where most of them reside—are driven, hands-on, and very smart people. They're not bad or mean. They just cut through things with a chainsaw as opposed to a butter knife. That's how they get things done.

Maybe you're one of those people. If that's your style, that's fine, as long as you know it and it works for your brand.

The Wunderkind

My first job at Turner was to manage the advertising for its fledgling network, TNT. Farrah Fawcett was starring in the TNT-original movie *The Margaret Bourke-White Story,* which profiled the famous *Life* magazine photographer. Farrah was using her own photographer, the legendary Herb Ritz, to do the movie poster's key art. My job was to select the photo, retouch it to Farrah's specifications, and create a headline. Late one night at the office, I received two phone calls. The first was from Farrah's agent, asking for additional retouching on the poster, which I had to refuse. The next came from TNT's president, Scott Sassa, a thirty-year-old wunderkind. Scott was furious.

"Why did you say no?" he demanded.

"Because we have no more money in the budget for re-touching."

"Shut up! Shut the *fuck* up! This is Hollywood! Don't you get it? Just give the agent what she wants!"

"If I retouch that neck anymore, she won't have one!"

"Did you hear me?"

"But I . . ."

"Shut the fuck up and *listen* to me. Just *do* it!"

"Scott—" But he slammed down the phone.

And I burst into tears.

The next day Scott asked me to lunch. He was funny and intelligent, and I hung on his every word. He never mentioned our conversation from the night before. When the check came I looked at him squarely and said, "I thought you'd either apologize or fire me."

"For what?" he said. He seemed genuinely surprised.

"Never mind." And then I took a deep breath and said, "I find you intimidating as hell, Scott!"

To which he answered, "Good."

Like all great people brands, Scott had decided long ago what tone and manner of communication he wanted to project. He'd established a *style,* negative as it could be. What did he have to gain from being so intimidating? He got people to work incredibly hard to avoid ever seeing their own heads on the chopping block. I worked for Scott for two more years and he was a pussy cat with me, never even raising his voice to me again. Because I never gave him any reason to.

Today, ten years later, Scott runs NBC and is worth zillions.

She's Gotta Have It!

Believe me, I'm not suggesting you emulate Scott Sassa's style. What I am saying is that you absolutely have to *have* a style.

As important as packaging is, **Presentation** may be even more critical to your success as a brand. Why? While packaging is about the external stuff, how you look, the dressing for the marketplace, presentation is about how you express what's inside—in your tone, communication style, and attitude. This is your unique "voice," not just how it sounds, but the **Power** behind it.

Scott Sassa's do-it-my-way style, his behavior toward associates and subordinates are all part of how he expresses his personal power to his audience. On the other hand, my mentor Brandon Tartikoff conveyed his power through his quiet strength, creative spirit, and lively wit. Both styles seem to work in Hollywood, where life is all about extremes.

To develop your own style in support of your brand, first know your personality—those visible, audible, behavioral aspects of your character.

> *Style is all about personal presence,*
> *that which frames your personality.*

All great product brands project a specific personality and perpetuate it in print, on television, and radio. The voice-over, music, key art, packaging, are all ways the brand showcases its personality. In order to imbue an inanimate product with personality, branding specialists will affiliate the product with a very recognizable human, on the proven theory that some of the human's *personality* will rub off on the product. For example:

- James Earl Jones is the VOICE of CNN. He sounds solid and authoritative, exactly what CNN is and wants to project.

- Cybill Shepherd, the spokeswoman for Mercedes, personifies "the good life." She appears carefree and yet elegant, just the way *you'd* feel driving in a Mercedes.

- Bill Cosby is to Jello Pudding what Mom is to apple pie.

- Elizabeth Hurley is an incredibly beautiful woman, but more important for her job as the Estee Lauder girl is that she projects an air of sophistication, sensuality, and great style. What does it say about *you*, if you use Estee Lauder products?

- Ralph Lauren has created a personality for his products by using models with a certain timeless, old-money, WASP "look" that communicates an aspirational life in idyllic surroundings.

- Some companies use surrogate people (Tony the Tiger, the Pillsbury Doughboy) to fill in the personality gap.

How do you communicate your personality? What's *your* style? Do you sparkle? Are you enthusiastic, interested, involved? Do you demonstrate your creativity or your competence in action and word? Are you curious, earnest, self-deprecating, sure of yourself, steady, clever, or adventurous—and *how* do you show it? Do your values shine through what you do and say? When you're comfortable in your skin, your inner light does shine through—and that light illuminates you and everyone in your presence.

Maya Angelou

Maya Angelou is one remarkable brand whose inner light attracts a diverse and devoted audience. Her presentation is a dramatic, exuberant expression of strength and pride in her own humanity and in ours. Her style is like gospel music—it comes from the heart and celebrates the spirit. And this very great, even spiritual presence evolves from a lifetime of struggle, and hurt, and an intimate knowledge of the darker, harder sides of life. "Fear brings out the worst thing in everybody," she has said.

Traumatized as a child, Maya was mute for five years. Afterward, she became devoted to school, to books, and the church. She was San Francisco's first black streetcar conductor and learned to cook Creole and supported herself as a chef.

Maya grew into herself, and is still becoming herself. Her presence is very much Mother Earth and the same time it is spirit mother.

An interesting past builds
a strong platform for great presence.

Count on your life's experience to ultimately develop inner confidence and comfort.

Sling Some Attitude, Girl!

Another way of talking about personal style is to talk about attitude. When the queen of attitude, ex-Texas governor Ann Richards, spoke at the Women in Leadership conference in San Francisco last year, she repeated Woody Allen's observation that 80 percent of work is showing up. She said, "You may feel so ground down in your job that you don't want to go to work. I'm telling you that you've got to show up."

And I'm telling you that you've got to show up with a killer attitude. It doesn't matter how good you look, if you're bored or bummed out you might as well have chicken pox. No one will want to come near you. When I call on a client or go to a trade show I put on my game face. It radiates interest, energy, good humor. I even put on that face for a conference call.

I'm not asking you to be fake. I'm asking you to open your heart. You may not be feeling energetic or in a great mood, but you know how dressing up can make you feel more together, more confident, more in charge? Well, arriving with the right attitude can change everything. If you act interested, you're very likely to get interested. If you act energetic, you'll attract energy. If you're good-humored, everything lightens up. "The only difference between a bad day and a good day is attitude," says motivational speaker Keith Harrell.

Attitude is about taking a stand,
having an opinion,
not being middle-of-the-road.

In order to help television networks and Web sites zero in on the attitude they want their brands to project, I create a list of adjectives that define that brand's personality. I call it an "attitude analysis." I'm as specific as possible. To say that Comedy Central has a sense of humor would be too vague and wouldn't tell the audience enough about where the network really stands on comedy. So here's an attitude analysis for Comedy Central as I see it:

Comedy Central is	*Comedy Central is not*
irreverent	silly
big-city	small-town
Ben Stiller	Don Rickles
original	imitative
clever	intellectual
entertaining	educational
unexpected	the same old thing
risk-taking	conventional
South Park	Jelly Stone Park
politically incorrect	P.C.

A couple of years ago, I worked on the brand strategy for the Professional Golf Association's Web site, PGA.com. This is how I identified its attitude:

PGA.com is	*PGA.com is not*
exclusive	exclusionary
professional	amateur

informative	chest-beating
instructional	arrogant
entertaining	flashy
engaging	smothering
inside	institutional
high-tech	slow-moving
substantial	trivial
clubby	lah-di-dah
personalized	impersonal

If you read each line above from left to right, you'll find the fine line that can never be crossed. Attitude analyses work similarly for brand people:

Laura

Laura is a high-energy people-pleaser, and sometimes her enthusiasm prevents her from saying "no." Often she finds herself working longer hours and taking on extra responsibilities at work with little payoff in appreciation or compensation. Then her enthusiasm turns to bitterness and dissatisfaction.

Laura is struggling with a kind of Catch-22: Her work energizes her and that energy can send her over the edge. She'll need to establish a balance she doesn't have now in order to get her energy to work for her instead of against her. Part of building her brand will be establishing a new attitude toward her work that's more respectful to herself. Borrowing from Coco Chanel, Laura will recite this mantra whenever she's moved to cave in: "Refusal is elegance."

This is Laura's newly constructed attitude analysis, a kind of chart for the behavioral modification she intends to develop to benefit her brand:

MAKE A NAME FOR YOURSELF

Laura is	*Laura is not*
positive	moody
balanced	out-of-whack
strong	a pushover
compassionate	emotional
a peacemaker	an anarchist
loyal	impatient
conscientious	sloppy
hardworking	workaholic
a teacher	a caretaker
accessible	intimidating
real	fake

Begin thinking in similar terms about yourself. What personal style do you want to project? What personality traits do you want to banish from your brand? You'll have the opportunity to create such a list for yourself in the exercise section of this chapter.

She's Got Something: The Charisma Factor

BAM! Seemingly out of nowhere, **Emeril Lagasse** has risen to celebrity status as a TV chef who loads on carbs and cream. **Marian Wright Edelman** receives media attention as well as celebrity and political backing for the Children's Defense Fund, while other worthy causes can't find a spotlight. **Judge Judy** rules the TV courtroom with an iron gavel that attracts armchair jurors in droves.

What do these three people have in common? Charisma! Elvis had it, J.F.K. had it, Oprah has it, Tina Turner has it, and so does Bill Clinton.

A lot of people think charisma is something you're born with—and they're right. But what not everyone knows is that we're *all* born with it. Whether or not we all *use* it is another question.

Some people say that charisma is a divine gift, a kind of spiritual power or personal quality that enables the one who has it to influence or command authority over others. News flash:

We are all charismatic people.
We've all received the same divine gift.

Charisma can be thought of as a magnetic element of the authentic self. When you allow your true self to open to your audience, your magnetism draws them to you. It's not so much a matter of your putting something across to them, but of your being open to receiving something *from* them, mainly their interested attention and positive response, even their love. If you absolutely revel in your audience and love their adulation, really thrive on it, you're probably considered very charismatic. And you're probably well aware that you receive much of your electricity from the audience itself, and reflect the crackle of their excitement back at them.

Elizabeth Dole

You may not agree with her politics, but Elizabeth Dole is one of those charismatic people who can deliver their message flawlessly. She's an out-in-front-of-the-podium person, passionate, articulate, and in charge.

Watch her. She leans in toward her audience. It's one of the ways she establishes the connection. She's smart, one of the first women to receive a law degree from Harvard, but she's not too smart for us. She talks just like we do, with a down-home twang. And she has a long-term, still sexy love affair with her husband, something we all wish for our futures.

Former president of the Red Cross, Liddy is a professional woman for professional women to relate to and a wife and lover for every other woman to admire. Although her run for the presidency was unsuccessful, the fact that she received so much support is a credit to her powerful brand.

*The successful brand is
constantly attentive to its audience.*

If there is a murmur of discontent within the target audience, the brand picks up on it and responds with something that's meant to comfort the audience and restore connection. The connection is what earns brand loyalty. So how do you connect with your target audience?

- SEE YOUR AUDIENCE. I mean really see them. Take a moment. Take a few breaths. Check the eyes of your audience, whether you're at the podium, in a meeting, or at a cocktail party. Are their eyes wandering, are they sneaking peeks at their watches, are they coughing or fidgeting, talking on their cell phones, checking their pagers? The ability to read your audience is critical to presentation. I think women are better at this than men. I think we are naturally a little more attentive. We notice more what's going on outside of us. We watch for signs that we might be losing our audience.

- LISTEN TO YOUR AUDIENCE. If you're present when the audience enters the room, you can observe a lot about them, including their sound. ***Check the audience's pulse for vital signs of success.*** Are they buzzing? A good sign. Are they silent, murmuring, boisterous? You can fathom an audience's mood based on visual or aural clues, and this lets you know exactly how you should be with them. Presenters will often try to mingle with an audience before beginning a speech, in order to get a good close feel for where they're coming from.

- OPEN YOUR HEART TO YOUR AUDIENCE. Really open your heart. This what I mean by being receptive. If applause follows your introduction, focus on that expression of audience respect and appreciation. Let a feeling of the audience's warmth roll over you before you begin to speak. After your presentation, if they applaud, take their approval to heart. Accept it. Take it in. Don't rush off the stage immediately. Love them for loving you. Your audience doesn't always applaud to show its approval. Be receptive to the appreciative looks and nods, the pat on the back, the congratulations.

Body Language: Presenting Yourself with Confidence

Sure, how you look—your outerwrap—is important, but presentation has more to do with how you move (or stand or sit), how you sound, the degree of charisma you bring to the table, your attitude, and to a significantly lesser degree *what* you say.

What you say is often the least of it.
How you say it is so much more.

Making an Impression

For instance, at a retreat in Arizona, I once had the job of demonstrating for TNT's executive staff what the company was offering our cable operators as a way of marketing the network at the local level. This was not especially scintillating material. Basically, we sent out a monthly support kit with print and television ads that the affiliate could customize for its particular market, and various press releases.

My challenge was to make walking through this box exciting to a room of one hundred people in shorts dying to get poolside.

I borrowed a girlfriend's red strapless ball gown and long white gloves. Another girlfriend lent me gobs of rhinestones. I entered the room like Queen Elizabeth, dripping with rhinestones, my head high, gaze straight ahead. I walked slowly from the back of the room, through the audience, to the front. In my hands, I held the monthly cable kit as if it were the Holy Grail.

Meanwhile, champagne was being passed throughout the room.

When I got to the front of the room, I announced, "Welcome to a *formal* presentation of Turner's Affiliate Marketing Kit." Jaws dropped and ears opened.

It's said that visuals count for more than half of the emotional impact of any presentation. Motivational workshop leader Mary Goldenson, Ph.D., estimates that appearances count for 68 percent of one's presentation, whether in a job interview, or in a situation where you're delivering a speech or proposal to an individual or to a group.

And every bit as important as the package is what you *do* with the package, and what the package does for you. In other words, how do you present yourself? Do you slouch? Do you fidget? Do you stand tall inside your wrapping? Do you carry your package and yourself with pride? Does your package instill you with confidence, make you feel powerful, bold, in charge? Body language, how we move or stand or sit *inside* our package, speaks volumes without a word being spoken.

So what volumes are you communicating? Analyze your presentation. Ask your brand advisers to give you the once-over. Ask them for complete honesty. Because they are your trusted friends they'll most likely be kind about how they offer criticism. Ask them:

- What impression do I make? You may be surprised with the feedback. I have a friend who always looks as if she's about to cry. She's a very happy person, it's more the shape of her eyes than her expression that makes her look so sad. But that look causes people to want to take care of her, to make sure she's okay. She never realized why people were so solicitous of her until she discovered this about herself.

- How do I move? What does my body language say?

- What do my looks communicate about me?

Diane Sawyer

What kind of impression does this distinctive woman make? Diane Sawyer's look says "girl next door" and "all-American." Her serious approach to current events projects concern, intelligence, compassion.

Her southern roots are part of her allure and part of her presentation. Although she's lost the accent, she retains the rhythm of a southern belle. She knows exactly when to pause and just where to stress a word. She shows no hard edges like many women in the highly competitive field of broadcast journalism (Maria Shriver and Christiane Amanpour come to mind). Diane's presentation is soft and feminine, while at the same time smart and competent.

Let's Go to the Videotape

Videotape yourself. Make a production of it. Grab a friend and conduct a phony interview for taping purposes. Dress for it. Or rehearse your speech in the mirror and tape it. Then review the tape with your focus group, your core friends, the women you trust, or your husband and children. How do you look—terrified or confident, prepared, relaxed? How do you *wear* your clothes? Do you smile? Does it seem as if you're actually *listening* to the interviewer?

What's your personal method of connecting with an audience? Are you a behind-the-podium speaker like Bob Pittman, CEO of America Online, or is your brand more like Elizabeth Dole's or Bill Gates's or Bill Clinton's—in *front* of the podium. (Clinton, master of the "town meeting" format, was one of the *first* politicians to make a big deal of stepping out from behind the podium.) If you wear glasses, think about getting contacts or the LASIK corrective eye surgery. If you wear glasses, especially tortoiseshell frames, the audience won't be able to see your eyes and it'll be that much more difficult for them to connect with you. Remember the eyes are the window to the soul. In fact, any block or barrier like glasses, the podium, or a sheaf of notes between yourself and your audience may block that magnetic current that you absolutely want to develop with them.

Emily

When Emily returned to work with a brand strategy in hand for becoming a fashion securities expert, networks like MSNBC and CNN came knocking on her door asking for forecasts.

Emily was a savvy self-marketer. She knew success required she be comfortable talking in front of a camera. She knew she wanted to come across as knowledgeable, and yet still be able to talk in layman's terms for the general public. Together with her husband, she constructed some tough questions and he videotaped her answering them.

To her surprise, Emily noticed that she used lots of "ums," and that she talked with her hands in a way that was distracting. She didn't hesitate to seek out a presentation specialist for counseling. Practice cleaned up her act and upped her style quotient considerably.

Your presentation style should project a long-term, going-somewhere brand that's all about success.

Carry Yourself Like a CEO

- STAND TALL: Height communicates authority. If you're tall, accentuate it. If you're not, learn to stride with confidence.

- WALK RIGHT IN, SIT RIGHT DOWN: When you enter a room, don't hesitate in the doorway or poke your head into the room first. Remember, you belong! And if you have a choice, choose any upright chair over a sofa, which can swallow you up in a single gulp.

- PASSIONATELY ENGAGE: Know these expressive tools: Wide eyes demonstrate interest. A *very* gentle nod indicates understanding, agreement, approval. When you lean forward your intensity and passion come across. (*Watch* how Hillary Clinton *listens* when someone else is talking.) It goes without saying that the gesture doesn't substitute for what it represents, but with practice, using these positive and powerful physical communicators can become a natural way of expressing interest, understanding, passion, and so forth. P.S.: If you're very attractive, you've got to go out of your way to be engaging, otherwise you'll be perceived as intimidating, or worse, stuck up.

Pump Up the Volume

Your sound is second only in importance to your appearance, so give your brand a powerful voice. Mary Goldenson attributes 20 percent of a speech's effectiveness to its tone, pitch, or pace.

Do you mumble? Do you swallow your words or whisper? Are you a speed speaker? Is your voice shrill, or nasal, or monotonous? Do you have a weird laugh? Unusual speech patterns? All of these things can have a negative effect on your brand. While they can prove to be obstacles, they shouldn't be permanent. Voice or speech lessons are an inexpensive enough investment in your brand's future.

It's not always an uphill battle. Mary Beth has a charming Georgia accent that works to her advantage. Emily's no-nonsense, in-a-hurry New York style comes across as authoritative and on-the-move, both great qualities for her brand to project.

Developing a voice of confidence instills confidence. Learning to modulate your voice makes everything you say more interesting. Lowering your voice a notch can add authority to what you say and it will also help you slow down. A voice coach can teach you how to make some very simple, small adjustments in your usual speech that will have a profound effect on your presentation.

Remember that your telephone voice is part of how you present yourself to the world. And because when you're on the phone your caller doesn't have the benefit of the visuals that can compensate for a deficit in the sound department, the voice becomes even more important than when you're having a conversation in person.

Sound Advice

- LISTEN TO YOURSELF: Sit down with a tape recorder and read aloud. Try an article from the business section of your newspaper, or your favorite columnist. Play back. How did you do? If you think you were great, then you won't mind sharing it with those wonderful people who are your brand advisers—your personal cheerleaders—whether they are close friends, or your husband, or your kids, or your business coach. What improvements do they suggest?

- EVALUATE YOURSELF AS STORYTELLER: Next, record yourself in a short conversation with a friend. Try telling your friend about the concept of branding, and what we're doing in this book. Listen for ums, ers, or other hesitations. Listen for word tics, words that you overuse. Do you sound stilted? Does your enthusiasm come across in your voice?

- SPEAK WITH A SMILE: If you smile when you answer the phone, your smile will shine right through the lines. If you're smiling you'll sound as if you couldn't be more delighted to be talking to the person on the other end. An upbeat phone personality communicates self-assuredness, personal comfort, and a positive outlook.

Be a Wordsmith

My father is a stickler about good grammar. When I was growing up, he corrected my English constantly—which embarrassed and irritated me to no end.

Another important image-maker to my dad was vocabulary. He would make me learn a new word from the *Reader's Digest* list every week. I had to say the word out loud and use it in a sentence. Now, I pepper my grammatically correct conversation and writing with interesting, descriptive words like *quagmire* and *euphemism*. When people hear me speak or read my writing, I am perceived to be well educated, which only serves to enhance my brand.

While my father's prodding annoyed me, learning to communicate properly has been a most valuable tool for my success. I strongly encourage you to drop the colloquialisms and street English that your peers may embrace, and present your intelligence and sophistication when you communicate.

Go Public

According to the *Wall Street Journal,* excellence in communication is the single most desired quality in the corporate and business world. And the more people you're able to touch, the more valuable your brand. This is true whether the brand is Sony or you—yet many women are hesitant to seek the wider playing field. According to Dr. Debra Condren, founder and director of Women's Business Alliance (tagline: "Women Empowering Women to Grow Their Businesses"), 75 percent of women in business would turn down the opportunity to speak to a group if it was offered to them.

I once saw a poll that rated the things in life people are most terrified of doing. The second biggest fear was of dying. Do you want to guess what the biggest fear was?

You got it. Public speaking.

I used to be among the 75 percent who'd just say no if asked to speak to a group, and I can really appreciate why we hang back. Sheer terror, right? Totally unrelated to the situation. My friend Joanne's heart used to beat so hard in her chest when all she had to do was introduce herself. "I'm Joanne. I'm an architectural assistant at Lowe, Cambden & Frieh," would be enough to send her adrenaline soaring. It's scary because we know that people are judging us and we're not sure what their verdict is. The lump in the throat, flushed cheeks, heart palpitations, stuttering are all symptoms of that unsureness.

When I first thought of developing personal branding for women, my coach, Mariette, encouraged me to learn how to speak in front of groups. If I was going to be true to my mission statement and wanted to share branding techniques to empower women, it would be far more efficient to do so with groups of women than one at a time, by appointment only.

I could see it was important to my brand, so I enrolled in a public speaking course at UCLA night school, and at the end of the eight-week course I stood up in front of one hundred women and ran my first workshop.

Even though I have a talent for performance, even though I've taken classes and know some tricks and techniques for public speaking, I still get nervous before making a presentation to the head of a network. Nervousness is not a success-maker. Nervousness is not what I want to project. Confidence, competence, professionalism, and energy are. So the night before any presentation I rehearse it in my mind exactly as I hope it will go. I picture it completely. I see myself walking through the door. I know exactly what I'm wearing. I imagine being introduced around the table. I imagine everyone in the room and what they look like. If I don't know who will be there, I make up a cast of characters. I visualize laying my portfolio down on the polished conference table. I imagine what I'm going to say, and how they're going to respond. I try not to let any negative thoughts into this fantasy. I want to walk away from that meeting with a new account, and I do in my imagination.

In this way, on the day of the meeting I'm prepared for the best to happen, and it frequently does. Before I step into the conference room for real, I put on what I call my "game face," and then I have a mantra I repeat, and this is it:

"No one in this room is a stranger."

I say that sentence two or three or twenty times, and then I'm *on*.

Learn to become comfortable speaking to large groups of people. Just do it. It's amazing how you transform yourself into a brand leader when you stand up in front of a group of people. And that's just the perception you need to move up in the ranks. Not only can you learn to speak to an audience with confidence, you can learn to have a great time doing it.

You don't necessarily have to use a script to give a talk. And memorizing a speech is always dicey. So try something radical.

The Promotion Cocktail

Not long ago, I was asked to participate in a panel discussion on effective promotion partnerships—as when Burger King teams up with Pokémon to give away toys at their fast-food restaurants. Instead of putting together a boring PowerPoint presentation, I presented a "promotion cocktail" to the other panel members. I put on an apron and squeezed oranges "for the juiciest ideas." I poured the juice into a martini shaker and added sugar "to sweeten the deal." Then I added vodka "to get the contract signed." Finally, I served the drink to the other panelists—in glasses that sported Big Fish Marketing's logo. (Never stop branding!) We went on to conduct a lively discussion on promotion partnerships.

The whole trick is in making the connection with your listeners. *Speaking is a contact sport.* Your audience is almost always going to be rooting for you, eager to be entertained or informed by whatever you've come to tell them. They're hardly ever the hard sell you fear. Try workshops, Speaking Circles,[1] books on the subject. Hire a speaking coach. Have faith in yourself.

You don't have to be a brilliant wordsmith to dash off a line or two by E-mail, but you do need the basics to write and speak clearly. If you don't have them, get them. A business coach should be able to help you with this, or direct you to a specialist.

Think on Your Feet

Whether you're presenting yourself one-on-one at a job interview, or in front of an audience, or anywhere in between, who you are will be best expressed by your ability to think on your feet. How good you are at this has a lot to do with confidence, with the inner knowledge that you *can* do it. You develop that inner knowledge with experience, and life is full of opportunities to prove to yourself that you can think quickly, that you can reach out and grasp opportunity when it presents itself, that you can turn something bad into something good.

When confronted by adversity,
real character is determined.

Mary Beth

Mary Beth had set up several interviews during a weeklong visit she made to Los Angeles as part of her exploratory work for her new career. When she arrived at one of these interviews, she discovered that she had left her portfolio in the back of the cab. And then when she was ushered into a conference room expecting to meet only the person she had arranged the meeting with, she found a group of six studio executives eager to talk to her about designing Web sites for their movies.

She described her mishap to the group, and asked them to please close their eyes and practice "theater of the mind." Then she proceeded to describe every piece of her missing-in-action portfolio.

She made a big impression on her audience that day, and by the time she returned to New York the following week, they had E-mailed her an offer. And before that, a very nice cab driver left a message on Mary Beth's voice mail that he had her portfolio and could make arrangements to drop it at her hotel.

She thought, "L.A. really is the City of Angels."

Step 7 Exercises:
Refining Your Brand's Presentation

1. *Try to put words to your personality and attitude.* What are you and what are you not? Create a list of adjectives that you want your brand to project, and a list that you don't want to project.

_____is   _____is not

_____   _____

_____   _____

_____   _____

2. *How do you look? How do you sound?* Produce a video of yourself in various situations. Dress for it. Rehearse an interview with a friend. Stand at a podium and deliver a speech. Watch yourself in a relaxed situation at home or outdoors. How do you come across in different situations?

   • Do you look comfortable?

   • How do your clothes look on you?

   • How's your posture?

Listen to yourself: Record your voice reading aloud, and then in an unrehearsed conversation with another person or people. What needs work?

   • tone quality (too shrill, nasal, quiet, etc.)?

   • Do you hem and haw?

   • pacing (too fast/too slow)?

   • How do you sound?
     stilted/enthusiastic/hesitant/confident . . .   (CONTINUES)

Try to put words to what comes to mind when you hear yourself.

_____

_____

_____

3. *Become a public speaker.* This is something you *must* learn to do. You don't have to make a career of it, but you do have to put your brand out in front of people to make it a success. So enroll in a class. Do it with a friend. But do it.

Devise a Plan and
Get on with It

*T*here was a period in my life when I didn't have a plan and it felt to me like wandering in the desert. I hungered for approval, acceptance, and understanding. I didn't realize that these goals required careful, focused, thoughtful planning followed by careful, focused, thoughtful action. Somehow I imagined that success just happened.

Well, sometimes it does, but it's rare. We usually have to work for success. And the work usually requires more than being a good girl and telling people what you know they want to hear. This chapter is all about laying out your plan for success.

In order to facilitate your brand plan, care, and maintenance program, it will be very helpful to buy a notebook that you can think of as your brand planner. Brand planning will include a marketing plan, a financial plan, and a timetable for launching. For this reason, your book should contain:

1. loose-leaf pages in which you can keep notes on strategy, short- and long-term goals, and for periodic reviews of how

things are going in general (a kind of brand equity evaluation on yourself);

2. a calendar that will allow you to track your "countdown to launch" as well as schedule appointments; and

3. a records section that will let you keep an overview of your budget and a running financial accounting of your business expenses.

Laying Out the Brand Planner

Designate a page in your planner for your **key attributes.**

Enumerate your **goals.**

Include your **brand description,**

And your **tagline.**

On a page by itself, as if it were a dedication—which it is—record your **mission statement.**

Fill a page with notes on your **target audience:**

- Who are they?

- Where will you find them?

- What do you want them to think/say about you?

How you describe yourself and your goal within these categories today will evolve into a new description over time. It's self-esteem–building to keep a record of your brand's changes, and equally important to manage those changes in a way that's consistent with the heart and soul of your brand and your overall plan for its growth.

Any brand strategy is constructed around the specifics What, When, Where, Why, and How, so also dedicate a page to a concise outline of those formative questions.

Jillian

WHAT: Reposition self as business manager for small companies

WHEN: Immediately

WHERE: Marin County, California

WHY: To achieve independence and more income

HOW: Through aggressive public relations efforts and rainy-day savings of $2,000 for initial company investment

Another important part of any brand plan consists of analyzing your risk factor (what if you don't succeed) vs. your responsibilities. In other words, don't quit your day job if the rent's due next week and it's going to take you months to get your first singing gig. In Jillian's profile, she calculates her R&R as follows:

RESPONSIBILITY: Sharing the greater financial obligation for household and lifestyle

RISK: Going into debt. If unsuccessful at finding two clients within first three months of severance, Jillian would have to look for full-time bookkeeping work "over the hill," an hour's commute from her rural home.

The opening pages of your planner, in which you define key attributes, goals, brand description, etc., are designed to help you maintain focus on your brand's *content.* The What/When/Where/Why/How and R&R represent the *context* for your brand.

Mary Beth

WHAT: Re-create brand as Web site designer

WHEN: Immediately

WHERE: Los Angeles, CA

WHY: To achieve financial success through art

HOW: By getting in the door at top Web site development firms and movie studios

RESPONSIBILITY: To be self-supporting

RISK: Loss of credibility with parents; big setback emotionally. If she fails to find a full-time job as a Web designer, Mary Beth will have to freelance until she builds a substantial portfolio. As a fall-back, she's also qualified as an advertising account executive.

The Grand Brand Scheme

The *How* part of your brand strategy should be a solid marketing plan. This is the platform from which you'll launch yourself toward your goal. Marketing consists of three basic areas—publicity, advertising, and promotion—and there are several different categories of promotions.

Publicity

As a new brand in a competitive marketplace, even without a huge bankroll, you can discover and maximize plenty of free publicity and public relations opportunities to let people know you're alive. Editorial coverage has the added power of being more credible than paid advertising and carries a moral stamp of approval that advertising doesn't. (In terms of dollars and cents, editorial coverage in print media is estimated at three times the value of paid advertisements of the same size.)

Publicize everything your brand accomplishes: When you hire an assistant, when you land an account, when you publish a book, when you win a lawsuit, when you change locations. Your objectives in publicizing your brand are to create visibility and a strong word-of-mouth. Your strategy could be as extensive as hiring a professional publicist, or as simple as asking your mentor to put in a good word for you.

Emily

Emily thought about hiring a professional publicist, but after a pep rally–type gathering of her six core friends, and with her natural New York chutzpah, thick skin, and sense of humor, she got on the phone and aggressively pitched herself to the media. She also became even more visible in the world of fashion, attending fashion shows and keeping in close contact with publicly held fashion companies. She outlined her objectives as follows:

- To establish relationships with key journalists, which would be instrumental in getting her appearances and articles.

- To gather financial news on the fashion world to feed several stories a week to the press.

She followed up any bites she got from journalists with a press kit she put together containing a bio and head shot inside a highly stylized folder with matching envelope, reprints of articles, and eventually a VHS tape with highlights of her television appearances.

Jillian

It's tough to change perceptions, but that's what Jillian had set out to do: to reposition herself from backroom bookkeeper to business manager. She called a two-man public relations firm she'd heard good things about, and convinced them to trade services. She'd handle their billing and receivables for three months if they'd pitch her new business as newsworthy to local papers and business journals during the same time period.

The PR efforts positioned Jillian as an expert in the economics of small businesses. Within the month she was being quoted in the county newspapers in articles about the realities of small-business management.

In month two, her local bank asked her if she could help them write a "Small Business Money Make-over" column for their monthly magazine.

Advertising

Any advertising you do to promote your brand should strive to accomplish the following:

- Communicate your promise and mission

- Address your key benefits

- Cut through the clutter with strong message and visuals

- Efficiently and effectively reach your target audience

- Make a positive impact and invite action

Some brand products spend two million dollars for a thirty-second spot during the Super Bowl. Now *that's* advertising. But when the brand being launched is a person, it's a whole other ballgame.

Laura made her advertising vehicle a newsletter. Mary Beth's was a Web site. Emily began sending internal E-mails that flowed through to interested clients, collating all of the day's news on fashion securities along with her analyses. That was advertising, too.

My company operates a weekly E-mail campaign called "Catch of the Day." It features a "fishism," which is actually a quote taken from the pages of this book. I sign off the E-mail with an invitation to my clients and prospects to contact us to help build their brands. The response has been phenomenal!

Personal brands like Jillian, who are starting their own businesses, might use more traditional advertising vehicles, such as newspapers or magazines. This requires capital, though, which is not always in great supply when you're starting out.

Paid Advertising	*Free Advertising*
Newspapers	E-mail
Magazines	Newsletters
Cable TV	Memos
Broadcast TV	Bulletin Boards
Radio	Letters
Internet	Website
Billboards	Fliers
Bus, subway, city bench	Word-of-mouth
Merchandise with your logo	Networking

Promotion

Promotions can also enhance your brand's desirability. When you set out to develop a promotion for your brand make sure that it gets you noticed in the right way. Each promotion that you execute on behalf of your personal brand should meet the following objectives:

- Generate brand awareness and build brand equity

- Reflect your brand's core values

- Reinforce your position

There are four basic categories of promotion: Value-added, Sweepstakes and Contests, Tie-ins, and Special events.

Value-added

A gift with purchase (GWP) or purchase with purchase (PWP) are examples of value-added promotions. They're designed to allow a sampling of your brand outside the boundaries of traditional business practice. For instance: Make an Estee Lauder purchase of $25 or more and receive a complimentary tote bag filled with makeup samples.

My friend Sally, an advertising copywriter, offers an incentive for new clients to work with her again by giving them a one-hundred-dollar rebate off their next project.

Sweepstakes and Contests

Sweepstakes are games of chance that require no purchase to play, versus contests, which are games of skill. These kinds of promotions ask the target audience to interact with a brand, while at the same time they can capture valuable database information.

Laura ran a contest in her newsletter (itself a promotional tool) that awarded a free hour's consultation to the winner of the paper's very popular "most embarrassing moment" feature. If you were starting a new business, you could run a "name my business" contest in your local newspaper. Even if you don't get a name out of it, you've got people talking and thinking about you, and in both cases, you've got their entries, with (at minimum) their names and addresses, the beginning of a valuable mailing list for the future.

Tie-ins

People brands can seek association with other people brands to strengthen their value. You can create a traditional partnership, or strike a strategic alliance with someone looking to influence the same target audience as you. If you're in corporate America, this might mean partnering with a supersmart co-worker on a project. If you're out on your own, you might sell your services alongside someone who complements your capabilities. I do this all the time in my business by outsourcing all the tasks I don't have in-house (such as printing and design) to the very best people in their fields, people whose own brands are solid. By working as partners, their reputations reflect on me, and mine does the same for them.

Prior to executing a promotion, it's a good idea to set up criteria for judging whether your idea should fly or die. Here's a checklist that I created for AXN, an action-adventure cable channel seen in Asia, Europe, and South America. Every promotion idea the company generates internally and externally is held up against this list:

Exciting

Fun

Attention-grabbing

Bold

Unique

Programming-related

Newsworthy

Feasible

Consistent with public relations efforts

Consistent with brand image

Create a similar list of your brand's key attributes and values, and ask yourself if your promotional efforts accentuate what you want them to. For instance, before Jillian mounted her promotion, she first asked herself, Does this promotion show people the following things about me?

my seriousness

my carefulness

my reliability

my discretion

my professionalism

Jillian

In order to break out of the strictly bookkeeping box and offer all of the services of a traditional business manager, Jillian needed a way to include tax services in what she offered her prospective clients. But Jillian isn't a CPA, and isn't considering going back to school to become one. Instead, she created a tie-in with the accountant whom she had sought out as a mentor. Both of them benefit from the coalition, being able to offer one another's services to their individual clients.

Special Events

Creating a community (a.k.a. a loyal audience) for your brand can happen when you host a special event. All across the country, Disney Channel hosts "Premiers in the Park," free screenings of Disney movies. Animal Planet has an enormous bus that goes from town to town rescuing animals caught in floods and fires, and educating families on how to keep pets safe.

My company hosts a "girls night out" for our female clients from different cable networks. It's always an unforgettable evening—a feast of great dishes and great "dish." Emily's monthly business alliance luncheons with guest speakers are a version of special events.

Mary Beth

Mary Beth got in touch with her mentor's two friends in Los Angeles, and they threw a party designed to introduce her to influentials in the entertainment industries who might supply leads. Jim, who had put the idea in her head to move to L.A., arrived with two plugged-in Web site developers. At the party she created an "altar" where guests could interact with her Web site. The next day she built a database with the business cards she had collected that evening. Her brand was out there. She was on her way.

Laura

Laura's proposal to her company's partners for a biannual workshop for managers is a special event that would be a showcase for Laura, as well as an opportunity for the execs to share their presentation skills, questions, and experiences. She had some great ideas for collaborative presentation "games," and outlined a broad-based curriculum, from audio to attitude, and from voice to video that could be carried out over the course of a daylong "retreat."

Crunching the Numbers

"I don't have the money" is many women's major justification for not investing in themselves (or their brands). *But no brand makes it without financial resources.* This concept has got to be factored into your brand plan for success.

You have to invest in yourself to succeed.

I'll bet I've heard "I can't afford to leave my job" a hundred times. I'm here to encourage you to look for how you might be able to afford it after all. Many great brands started out with little capital. Apple Computer's first lab was in a garage. Nike running shoes were originally made in a kitchen by pouring hot rubber on a waffle iron. Vision and faith made these companies great. Savvy planning made them prosperous.

You do what you have to do. Whether you're a teacher who wants to become a lawyer, a manager at a corporation who wants to start her own Internet business, or a house painter who wants to become a fine artist, you *can* find a way to make it happen if your heart is in it. You may have to keep your day job and carve out time at night or on weekends for building your dream. I know so many people who take night classes or have become weekend artists. You may have to beg and borrow. Don't let lack of money be an excuse for not starting.

My plan was to leave Turner Broadcasting to start my own agency when I turned thirty. As I approached that milestone, I got scared. I was living comfortably on a good salary, but I had zero savings. How was I going to make the leap without putting myself in jeopardy?

My first move was to invest in myself instead of Turner Broadcasting. Even before I gave my three-months notice, I cashed in the $10,000 in stock that I'd accumulated through the company's stock purchase plan. From those funds I spent $3,000 on a computer and printer. I spent another $3,000 for letterhead, business cards, and mailing labels.

$10,000.00	starting capital
3,000.00	computer equipment
3,000.00	business cards/letterhead

Do the math. With what was left over I had to install a phone system in my house, incorporate my company, buy office supplies, eat, and pay the mortgage until my first check arrived from either Discovery or Hanna-Barbera (the two clients I had secured before I left Turner).

Think, think, think about what it will take to launch your brand. There are always expenses, whether you're starting up a business, or entering or reentering the job market, or moving steadily up a corporate ladder. Try to anticipate every little financial requirement your brand will need—all your expenses, start-up and otherwise. These include packaging expenses, from business suit to portfolio; possible advertising costs to introduce yourself; office equipment and supplies if you're on your own; speech or writing teacher, publicist, business coach, financial adviser, physical trainer (part of care and maintenance costs), etc.

Enter all these in the record-keeping section of your brand planner. I have a friend who thought that leaving her six-figure job to start a cooking school out of her house was the ideal way out of the corporate grind. When she took a hard look at the numbers (for minor remodeling of her kitchen, finding students, kitchen supplies, school supplies, administration expenses, marketing costs, and so forth), she discovered that she'd be pulling in a whopping $12,000 a year after expenses.

Next!

The monetary calculation that goes into your business plan is necessary in order to ground yourself in reality. Once you know what financial backing you need, you can set your sights on manifesting it. By "manifest," I don't mean, "Poof! You've got money!" I mean look around and see where the resources you need are to be found, and then take the bold next step and go for it. Don't overlook what you can generate by saving. I began saving like crazy in the months before I left Turner. I began to eat home more, I became a thrift-store junkie. By the time I did leave, it wasn't exactly like stepping off a cliff, it was more like stepping off a cliff on a wing and a prayer.

Do you have investments? Ask yourself if it makes sense to trade them for the investment in yourself, like I did. Go to the bank for a loan. Find an "angel" investor. Ask a family member who can afford to invest in your future to make you a loan.

And don't forget to *ask the universe for what you want.* I'm not kidding: This is half of what success in any category is all about. Tell the universe, but don't neglect letting everyone else know what your aims are. For one thing, you'll elicit a lot of advice, which can serve as reality check points, important all along the road to success. Ask those people you respect to help you shape your capital-raising strategy.

Tell everybody what your dreams are because you never know where help will come from. Listen to the advice you solicit, but also trust yourself. If you've done the work, if you believe you're ready to step out or step up, even though you're scared, *do* it. Go for it. You can't win if you don't bet on yourself.

Mary Beth

Mary Beth borrowed $16,000 from the trust fund her grandfather had left her to carry her for three months. She enumerated her expenses this way:

driving car cross-country	$1,000.00
Web site setup costs	1,250.00
studio apt. in L.A (per month)	900.00
setting up new apt.: first/last/deposit	2,700.00
moving expenses	2,500.00
furnishings	1,000.00
updating portfolio expenses	100.00
business cards	500.00
$ for taking people to lunches (per week)	100.00
living expenses (per month)	1,000.00

*Brand success asks you to think about your brand in this very intense, obsessive way: writing it **down**, talking it **up**, putting it **out** in the universe to fulfill its destiny.*

Timing Is Everything: Countdown to Launch

I've recently launched a new brand extension. Evolution is a major part of my grand brand scheme, and one of the ways I'm evolving is by narrowing the focus of my companies, resources, and expertise into several different branded entities that specialize in specific areas within the digital world. Big Fish Marketing specializes in cable network marketing, Little Pond Productions has expertise in TV and Web based sweepstakes and contests, and a short ten months ago I launched FishNet, a company that specializes in Internet branding and marketing. Here's what I did to count down its successful launch:

WEEK ONE: Write brand strategy
Make list of potential clients
Book business lunches with contacts

WEEK TWO: Give designer logo assignment
Buy new laptop computer for general
manager
Network all computers

WEEK THREE: Set up schedule for upcoming trade shows
Put together portfolio
Write brochure copy
Review first round of logos

WEEK FOUR: Begin Web site development
Approve layouts for business cards,
letterhead
Schedule pitches with potential clients
Approve brochure layout

WEEK FIVE: Send press release with head shots to media
Finalize portfolio and sales brochures
Send E-mail to database to announce
company

WEEK SIX: Place follow-up calls to the media
All materials printed and delivered
Web site complete
LAUNCH! (party!)

Your brand launch may take longer. You may not be launching a
business, but a plan of action at work like Laura's, or a job search
like Mary Beth's, or a vertical move in your field like Emily's. Any
launch needs a similar kind of timetable. Use the calendar portion of
your brand planner to count down to launch.

Emily

WEEK ONE: Get head shots taken
Write bio
Select media kit folders with envelopes

WEEK TWO: Select head shot from proofs
Develop media contact list
Collate kits

WEEK THREE: Place calls to media
Create daily analysis of fashion-related
equities/funds

Give Your Brand Some Juice

In addition to containing your timetable for launching, the calendar portion of your planner will become studded with reminders. For example, you've got to nurture your target audience.

- Set aside *a day a month to call clients, to check in with your boss, to see what's up with colleagues or vendors, to be remembered by the people you want to be thinking about you.* (Make notes on every call. Keep a file on all your clients, colleagues, vendors, everyone who's important to your career.)

- If you depend on your car for work, you'll write in *scheduled maintenance* every four or six months, depending on your needs.

- *Résumés need to be fresh and should be revised at least yearly,* even if the change is minuscule. (This is true whether you're job hunting or happy as a clam in a company you hope to stay with forever.)

- Whether you live where there are four seasons, or only two, mark your calendar to remind yourself to do a *pre-season pack-*

age review. Buy a new lipstick, take clothes to the cleaners, resole shoes, add highlights, and so forth.

- Schedule *once or twice yearly market surveys,* during which you'll ask the $64,000 two-part question: *What does my target audience think of me? What do I want them to think?* Use performance reviews, fax-back surveys, questionnaire cards, or candid client meetings to determine where you stand.

Discipline Is a Means to Happiness

Think about it. No matter how feasible and realistic your plan for success, if you spend your workdays glued to talk shows eating bon-bons, or yacking with your girlfriends, or playing computer solitaire, you're very likely to fail.

Managing yourself, your product, your time, your family, the information you receive is a lot, but as CEO of your life, who else is going to do it? So if you're leaving the corporate world for the world of the entrepreneur, or if you're looking for your first job or your fifth, it means getting up every morning, getting into work mode, dressing the part, hitting the phone to dial for dollars, and going to appointments with potential clients or employers. If your goal is to advance yourself within your company, or improve yourself or your business, it means keeping your eye on the prize and constantly and consistently working toward that end.

Hey, no one said branding was easy. But take it from me, the rewards for this effort are huge.

Plan on Your Brand's Evolution

Have you ever seen an eighty-year-old who dresses in too-short skirts with too much makeup and Shirley Temple curls? It can be mortifying to hang onto a brand that's no longer appropriate. Just as people evolve gradually over time, so should their brands. For instance, Kellogg Company, demonstrating how it's grown up, recently introduced its first new Frosted Flakes ad campaign in fourteen years with a series of clever, very "new" looking, documentary-style television ads—still featuring their old star, Tony the Tiger. Mega retailer, Target, has evolved into a hip, twenty-first century brand by celebrating its products and reinventing its bull's eye logo. Now, it's cool to shop at Target.

Staying Power

> The following brands entered the marketplace in the 1920s: Baby Ruth, Oh Henry!, Mounds, Charleston Chews, Mr. Goodbar, Reese's Peanut Butter Cups, Bit-O-Honey, Butterfinger, Eskimo Pie, Hostess Cakes, Wonder bread, Peter Pan peanut butter, Welch's Grape Jelly, Kool-Aid, Wheaties, Rice Krispies, Howard Johnson's, Better Homes & Gardens, Betty Crocker, Safeway Stores.

Over their lifetimes the brands above have been through many changes. Some have changed their ingredients, some have gotten bigger, all have modified their packaging to stay appealing to current tastes and styles. Brand lifts have kept them young. It's called brand evolution.

Evolving your brand may mean adding products to your line (line extension), adopting new specialties, and/or getting better and better at what you do. You can have the pleasure of watching yourself develop if you're meticulous about keeping copies of your ever-changing résumé/portfolio.

If you're changing the direction or focus of your brand, do it gradually. Hold on to those qualities that have worked best for your career, and add to them, or play them up at the same time you're playing down the ones you're phasing out.

IBM, a big, conservative, old-line company, is getting hip by adapting to the Internet, turning its big computers into giant Web servers and electronic traders. That's evolution.

The Chivas Regal brand has sort of an elitist appeal that the company is trying to soften to make more accessible to a wider audience. Three decades ago they used the line "Give Dad an expensive belt" in their Father's Day advertising. Though they're marketing to a broader audience, they've maintained the witty/hip talk they're known for. Turn-of-the-twenty-first century advertising uses: "Sit back. Pour glass. Survey kingdom." They're evolving but they've kept what works.

Cher started out as Sonny-and-Cher and has grown into Cher over forty years, not reinventing herself but evolving over time. She made one big misstep in the nineties, hawking a line of cosmetics on infomercials. Her audience was appalled. She had gone from a hip diva to a street vendor and Cher admits it. She had joined a completely different category. Her career slid. This was devolution, not evolution, and it broke one of branding's most inviolate laws, that of consistency. Lucky for Cher, she caught herself in time and jumped back into the kind of outrageous, campy entertainment her audience loves her for.

Oprah Winfrey—my hero—made a decision in 1994 that would change her brand. Daytime talk shows were getting trashy, and even she was resorting to the sensational in order to keep up with the crowd. Her brand was slipping away from her. She decided to bring it back to basics—those core values we've been talking about. She held on to the qualities that mean the most to her—her interest in books, the importance of spirituality in her life—and she added her book club and featured uplifting and relevant discussions and interviews with people who are doing something with their lives. Meanwhile, Jerry Springer is still getting beat up on his set, and dysfunctional mothers and daughters are slugging it out on *Sally Jessy Raphael.*

Celebrate the Brand That Is You!

Successful brands celebrate their content and thrive on loyalty. Your personal brand requires no less of you than loyalty to its mission and a celebration of all that it stands for. This means staying interested in the health and welfare of your brand each and every day, keeping attuned to how it's received, and looking for opportunities to promote it. If you're sold on your brand and authentically communicate that fact with passion, you'll sell your target audience on yourself without selling your soul. But give yourself time. Don't switch strategies if things don't begin clicking right away. Brand equity takes time to establish, and when the brand is a person, it can be the joyful work of a lifetime.

Step 8 Exercises:
Strategizing for Your Brand's Success

1. BRANDING CHECKLIST

In everything you do in relation to your brand, ask yourself these questions:

- **Honesty:** Can I deliver what I'm promising? Am I over-hyping or overpromising?

- **Mission directed:** Is my mission integral in every action I take?

- **Fresh, different:** Have I tried something new lately? Taken a risk? Done it differently from the way it's been done before?

- **Quality:** Does my positioning as a brand meet the standards of quality I've set for myself based on my core values?

- **Targeted appeal:** Is my packaging and presentation appealing to my target audience?

- **Interactive:** Does my brand strategy engage my audience and inspire them to action?

- **Aggressively promoted:** Are my marketing tactics efficient and effective in creating awareness for my brand?

2. LAY OUT WHERE YOU'RE GOING

Just so you never get lost, the following will serve as the map of your intentions:

What:

When:

(CONTINUES)

Where:

Why:

How:

Responsibility:

Risk:

3. Lay Out Your Marketing Plan

Consider the marketing tools available to you. Use any or all to bring yourself to the attention of your target audience.

a. Publicity: Let the media know you exist and find you interesting.

b. Advertising: Let the rest of the world get to know your brand. Use any of the means below:

- Newspapers
- Magazines
- Cable TV
- Broadcast TV
- Radio
- Internet
- Billboards
- Bus, subway, city bench
- Merchandise with your logo

- E-mail
- Newsletters
- Memos
- Bulletin boards
- Letters
- Website
- Fliers
- Word-of-mouth
- Networking

c. Promotion: Give people an incentive to work with you by using one or more of the following tactics:

- Value-added
- Sweepstake or contest
- Tie-in
- Special event

4. CREATE YOUR FINANCIAL PLAN

Try to anticipate and itemize what your brand's goals require. If you're starting out in business for yourself or entering the workforce for the first time, there are one time or start-up costs that every brand needs. I've listed some universal costs below to get you started, but every list will be as unique as every brand, so elaborate on and personalize the following:

Item	*Cost*
rent	
phone/fax/computer	
résumé/portfolio	
business cards/letterhead	
transportation and car upkeep	
packaging (outerwear)	
presentation (for speech coach, etc.)	
marketing (for publicist, etc.)	
maintenance (membership at gym, etc.)	

5. MANIFESTING MONEY

Use this space to write down potential sources of revenue for building your brand.

- How much can you save, starting now?
- What savings do you already have to tap?
- What investments can you draw on, and for how much?
- Find an "angel" investor or venture capitalist.
- What family members can you approach for loans of how much?
- Check out the possibility of a bank loan.

(CONTINUES)

CREATE A TIMETABLE

How long do you give yourself to go from concept to accomplishment? How long from the time you decide you want a job, a raise, or a promotion until the day you get it? Start by laying out a weekly table of things to accomplish on the way to achieving your goal:

• Week One	• Week Five
• Week Two	• Week Six
• Week Three	• Week Seven
• Week Four	• Week Eight

7. KEEP YOUR BRAND CURRENT

Include notes in your calendar to "remind-me-to" do the following:

- Once a month, check up on your target audience.

- Every 4,000 miles, check up on your car (change oil, check maintenance).

- Revise résumé at least yearly.

- Pre-season package review.

- Once or twice yearly market surveys: How am I doing with my target audience?

- At least once a year, schedule something new, a class or workshop.

8. BRAND LIFTS

If you don't take care of yourself, your brand will suffer. Write down three things you'll do for yourself this month to make you feel wonderful. Next month do the same. Schedule brand lifts into your calendar. They're as important as anything you do at work.

_____

_____

_____

CONCLUSION:

The Next Step

I don't know how many business meetings I've attended that have ended with the rhetorical, "What's the next step?" Hundreds, definitely. Once the task force has met, sized things up, formed a plan, made its report, launched its program—what's the next step?

Just completing the eight steps outlined in this book pretty much guarantees that you're making a name for yourself, getting noticed, and being remembered. The next step for you might be to go back to the exercises at the end of each chapter and fine-tune your brand strategy so that you reveal the best and truest you. And if you haven't done so already, begin your brand journal to help you target what you want and how to achieve it. And when times get tough, you can come back to this book to remind yourself of what's important: living your passions, attracting meaningful projects, and forming and strengthening relationships with people who share your core values.

Sometimes it's hard to remember that there's a purpose to your precious life. It's way too easy to lose sight of the reality that you're here on this earth for a reason when you're sweating the details for your company's IPO, racing against deadlines, negotiating contracts, playing politics, or out there hustling for work.

The commercial world is tough, turf wars are commonplace, the competition can be brutal, and self-doubt *will* rear its ugly head.

But life is also shimmering with divine spirit. Believe it. Life is golden with possibility. Look for it inside yourself, and look outside, too. Use every means within your power to gather what blessings may lie within your grasp. Your reward will be the gift of freedom and self-expression, and everyone you work with will be rewarded, too, with the gift of your dynamic spirit.

Think of your challenges as lessons meant to move you closer to fulfilling your destiny. And if you lose your focus, if you get off track, *have a reference point for your soul to connect with.* This could be your mentor, your mission statement, your garden, your journal, your children, or prayer. It doesn't matter what you use to give you a direct line back to yourself, to your brand, as long as it works to return you there. You'll soon discover that every return trip to the deep well where your core values reside acts to empower your brand. Don't wait until you need replenishment to visit there. Go often and drink deeply.

A mentor of mine once told me that life is not a dress rehearsal. I know it's a cliché, but it's become that for a reason—it's true. This is it. When you don't move toward your goal, when you hang on to the past or only move in place, then you've put your life on hold and you may be tempting your true destiny to pass you by.

The net/net is that you can jump-start your destiny cycle by crafting a brilliant brand strategy that illuminates the real you. Go ahead, reinvent yourself, move and shake, explore new territory, do what you love, get noticed, be remembered, MAKE A NAME FOR YOURSELF.

Notes

Step Two

1. A. Mikaelian, *Women Who Mean Business* (Morrow, 1999), p. 43.

Step Three

1. Pierre Mornell, *Games Companies Play* (Ten Speed Press, 2000), from the manuscript.

2. *Ibid.*

3. Abby Ellin, "Bang Your Drum Loudly," *New York Times,* June 25, 1999.

4. Al and Laura Ries, *The 22 Immutable Laws of Branding* (Harper Business, 1998), p. 90.

Step Four

1. "These Women Rule," Patricia Sellers, *Fortune,* October 25, 1999, p. 120.

STEP FIVE

1. Hillary Stout, "The Front Lines: Start-Up That Uses Web to Reach South Asians Gets Boost from Mentor," *Wall Street Journal,* Feb. 5, 1999, p. B1.

STEP SIX

1. Pierre Mornell, *Hiring Smart! How to Predict Winners & Losers in the Incredibly Expensive People-Reading Game* (Ten Speed Press, 1998), pp. 92, 95.

2. From the label of "Newman's Own" Venetian Pasta Sauce.

STEP SEVEN

1. Transformational Speaking Circles is a trademarked term of Lee Glickstein, a nationally recognized coach, speaker, and authority on effective public presence and authentic speaking skills. His book, *Be Heard Now,* was published by Broadway Books in 1998.

Acknowledgments

With immense love and devotion
I dedicate this book to my daughter,
Roxanne,
and my husband,
Steven Roffer,
who remind me every day what true joy
it is to be a woman.

And with admiration I want to express my
appreciation to my father,
Robert J. Edelman,
who taught me how to close deals and create
long-lasting business relationships.

I would like to send my heartfelt thanks
to my best friend and sister,
Wendy Hardman;

New York's most amazing agent,
Barbara Lowenstein;
the ideal editor,
Lauren Marino;
my genius collaborator,
Doris Ober;
and the world's best business coach,
Mariette Edwards,
for challenging me to dig deeper and aim higher.

I'd also like to give a sweet embrace to my dear friends
Jay Welsh and Rae Terry,
who cheered me on and gave me hope,
and the five fabulous femmes who kept me on track:
Kim Deck,
Jolla Harris,
Annie Morita,
Sherri York,
and the undeniable
Kim Youngblood.

About the Author

As the premier brand strategist for the digital age, Robin Fisher Roffer develops brand-building marketing plans and promotional campaigns for launching television networks and Internet Web sites around the world.

Her flagship company, Big Fish Marketing, counts among its clients ABC, A&E, CNN, Comedy Central, Discovery Channel, Disney Channel, ESPN, Fox Family Channel, The History Channel, Lifetime Television, MTV, Oxygen, TBS, and Turner Classic Movies. She has contributed to the visionary launches of domestic cable networks TNT, TLC, FX, Game Show Network, and Animal Planet, as well as global brands like Asian action/adventure channel AXN, Sony Entertainment Television in India and Latin America, and Japanese channels SheTV for women, SF (Science Fiction), and ANIMAX, an all-animation channel.

Fisher Roffer worked with the legendary Brandon Tartikoff to launch three Web sites for America Online: Entertainment Asylum.com, Passion.com, and Electra.com, now part of Oxygen.com. She has also created marketing plans for Web sites like NHL.com, PGA.com, and eAgents.com, and developed Web sites for cable networks such as Turner and Fox Family Channel.

Little Pond Productions, Fisher Roffer's promotion company, is sought after for creating and executing cutting-edge cable TV and online sweepstakes and contests. And she has recently launched a third company, FishNet, which specializes in end-to-end brand-based solutions for the Web. The fledgling company has branded and built Web sites for Turner Networks, Fox Family Channel, Galavision, and Univision.

Fisher Roffer also uses her passion for television to leverage entertainment for a greater good, and is proudest of the accolades she's received for developing community outreach programs like Hanna-Barbera's "Radical Right Riders" bicycle safety program, The History Channel's "Save Our History: World War II Memorial," CNN's "Your Choice, Your Voice 2000," a campaign for the presidential election, TBS's "Goodwill Games Scholarship Competition," and Comedy Central's "Comedy RX," a hospital-based program promoting the healing power of laughter.

Fisher Roffer makes her home in Los Angeles, California, where she lives with her husband, Steven, their one-year-old daughter, Roxanne, and their dog, Saki.